THEOLOGY · PHILOSOPHY ·

ISEB
Independent Schools
Examinations Board

Theology & Philosophy

FOR COMMON ENTRANCE

Susan Grenfell
Michael Wilcockson

13+

DYNAMIC LEARNING

HODDER
EDUCATION
AN HACHETTE UK COMPANY

The Publishers would like to thank the following for permission to reproduce copyright material.

Photo credits

Acknowledgements

The Holy Bible, New International Version®, NIV®. Copyright© 1973, 1978, 1984, 2011 by Biblica, Inc.® Used by permission. All rights reserved worldwide.

Every effort has been made to trace all copyright holders, but if any have been inadvertently overlooked, the Publishers will be pleased to make the necessary arrangements at the first opportunity.

Although every effort has been made to ensure that website addresses are correct at time of going to press, Hodder Education cannot be held responsible for the content of any website mentioned in this book. It is sometimes possible to find a relocated web page by typing in the address of the home page for a website in the URL window of your browser.

Hachette UK's policy is to use papers that are natural, renewable and recyclable products and made from wood grown in sustainable forests. The logging and manufacturing processes are expected to conform to the environmental regulations of the country of origin.

Orders: please contact Bookpoint Ltd, 130 Park Drive, Milton Park, Abingdon, Oxon OX14 4SE. Telephone: (44) 01235 827827. Fax: (44) 01235 400401. Email education@bookpoint.co.uk. Lines are open from 9 a.m. to 5 p.m., Monday to Saturday, with a 24-hour message answering service. You can also order through our website: www.hoddereducation.co.uk

ISBN: 9781510422292

© Susan Grenfell and Michael Wilcockson 2018

First published in 2018 by
Hodder Education,
An Hachette UK Company
Carmelite House
50 Victoria Embankment
London EC4Y 0DZ

www.hoddereducation.co.uk

Impression number 10 9 8 7 6 5 4 3

Year   2022 2021 2020 2019

Cover illustration by Barking Dog

Illustrations by Oxford Designer and Illustrators and Integra Software Services

Typeset by Integra Software Services Pvt. Ltd., Pondicherry, India

Printed in India

A catalogue record for this title is available from the British Library.

Contents

Section 2 Philosophy

Section 1 Theology

What is theology?

Theology is the study of the nature of God and religious beliefs. In Christianity, one of the best ways of doing this is through studying the Bible. The first section of this book is about the Bible and what it tells us about God, the world and human beings. Theology is important because it helps people understand how a religion is put into practice. The stories in this part of the book show how God created the world, how human beings continually spoiled it, and God's plan to bring them back into a good relationship with him.

Starter
No one can really know God. Do you agree?

The Bible

The Bible is made up of many different books and is divided into two sections: **Old Testament** and **New Testament**. 'Testament' means covenant or agreement. The Old Testament is about the old covenant that God had with human beings, which he drew up with **Moses**, when he gave him the Law. The New Testament is about the new covenant, which was introduced by Jesus.

The first part of the Bible deals with God's creation of the world. It explains how the Jewish nation came into being through **Abraham**. It recounts the story of how Moses brought the Israelites out of Egypt, how God gave Moses the Ten Commandments and how they settled in Canaan, later called Israel.

▲ This famous mural is in the Sistine Chapel in Rome. It shows God and Adam reaching towards each other, which pretty well sums up the story of the Bible.

The next part records the achievements and failures of Israel's kings and commanders, such as **David**, their time in exile and their return to Israel. It also contains prophetic passages by prophets like Isaiah about the coming of a **Messiah**, whom Christians believe is **Jesus**.

The New Testament opens with the **life and teaching of Jesus**. It charts the beginning of Christianity and includes letters from early Christian leaders, which teach much of what now makes up the guidelines for Christian living. They are examples of how God continued to communicate with and work through his people and how theology developed as people tried to live Christian lives.

The Bible finishes with the book of Revelation – a unique book full of prophecies and visions – written by a man called John.

Topic 1

God's relationship with the world

In Topic 1 we look at the way God reveals himself to human beings and builds a relationship with them and the world. The topic includes both Old and New Testament stories; they all show that God is as active now as he was at the beginning, when he created everything. Christians believe Jesus is God's son and that he reveals the nature of God in his life and teaching. The stories explain how God wants people to behave towards him and towards each other. As you work through the chapters in this topic, think about how and why God gets involved with human beings.

Assuming God exists, what is he like?

Comparing the Old Testament to the New Testament, does God always work in the same way?

Does God know everything?

How does he get in touch with his world?

What would you say to God if you could meet him face to face?

Can God suffer?

Does God carry out miracles?

How do we know how God wants us to live?

Does God intervene in the affairs of the world?

How can we know anything about God?

How can we talk to God?

Is God always good?

Activity

In groups, discuss these questions. Which are the most important issues?

Come back to your answers at the end of your study of Topic 1 and compare what you think then with what you think now.

1.1 God the creator

The opening story in the Bible introduces one of the most important things about God. He is the **creator** of all things. The story appears in Genesis, a word that means origin or beginning. The events of the creation story are presented in the structure of a week – not in chronological order as we might expect if we were to write such an account today, but in a topical order. First is the creation of the regions: land, sea and sky. Second is the creation of what will dominate each region: the stars in the sky, the fish in the sea and the animals and human beings on the land. Lastly, when God has finished, he establishes himself as Lord of his creation. The seventh day is the triumphant finale when he 'rested'. The language of the story is poetic, expressing order and meaning with all things having their place and part to play.

This account is very different from other creation stories that were circulating in the Ancient Near East at the same time and Genesis 1 was probably written to counter them. Most people at that time believed that the world was ruled by malevolent chaos gods (beings who acted in evil and unpredictable ways), who placed no value on human life at all. The writer wanted to establish that the God of Israel was completely different. It was he alone who created the universe and human beings had a purpose and a destiny within it. He wanted to show that people were valued by God and that the whole of creation had a common connection to the creator. The position of the story at the very beginning of the Bible places God's divine plan for the world and for human beings right at the heart of the Bible story.

▲ According to the Bible, God is the creator of all things.

Genesis 1.1–2.4

Starter

Who made the world?

1 In the beginning God created the heavens and the earth. 2 Now the earth was formless and empty, darkness was over the surface of the deep, and the Spirit of God was hovering over the waters.

Day 1

3 And God said, 'Let there be light,' and there was light. 4 God saw that the light was good … 5 God called the light 'day', and the darkness he called 'night'.

Day 2

6 And God said, 'Let there be a vault between the waters to separate water from water …'. 7 And it was so. 8 God called the vault 'sky'.

Day 3

9 And God said, 'Let the water under the sky be gathered to one place and let dry ground appear.' And it was so. 10 God called the dry ground 'land', and the gathered waters he called 'seas'. And God saw that it was good. 11 Then God said, 'Let the land produce vegetation …' And it was so.

Day 4

14 And God said, 'Let there be lights in the vault of the sky to separate the day from the night …' 15 And it was so. … 18 And God saw that it was good.

Day 5

20 And God said, 'Let the water teem with living creatures, and let birds fly above the earth …' 21 So God created the great creatures of the sea and every living thing with which the water teems … and every winged bird … And God saw that it was good. 22 God blessed them and said, 'Be fruitful and increase in number …'

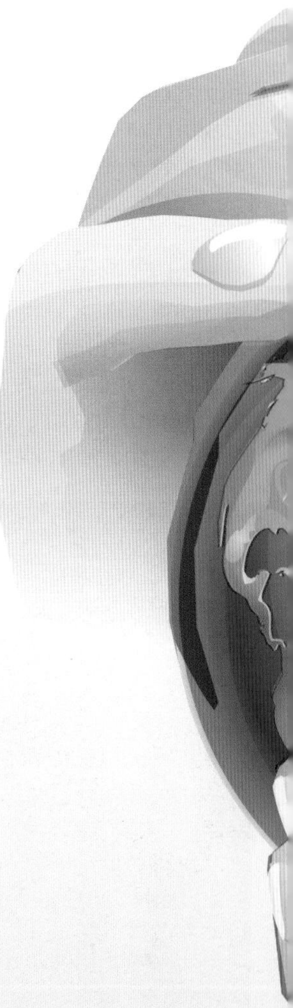

Day 6

24 And God said, 'Let the land produce living creatures ...' And it was so. ... And God saw that it was good. 26 Then God said, 'Let us make mankind in our image, in our likeness, so that they may rule over the fish in the sea and the birds in the sky, over the livestock and all the wild animals, and over all the creatures that move along the ground.' 27 So God created mankind in his own image, in the image of God he created them; male and female he created them. 28 God blessed them and said to them 'Be fruitful and increase in number; fill the earth and subdue it ... 29 I give you every seed-bearing plant on the face of the whole earth and every tree that has fruit with seed in it. They will be yours for food ...' 31 God saw all that he had made, and it was very good.

Day 7

2 God had finished the work he had been doing; so on the seventh day he rested from all his work. 3 Then God blessed the seventh day and made it holy....

Activity

Make a collage or a storyboard to show what God created on each day. Use pictures or drawings to illustrate it.

What do you know? AO1

1 Describe in detail what God created on the third day.

2 What were the sun, moon and stars for?

3 Describe what God did on the sixth day.

What do you understand? AO2

4 What do you learn about God from the way he created human beings?

5 What does God's provision for animals and humans tell us about his relationship with the world?

What do you think? AO3

6 What does it mean when it says 'God rested?' What might that imply for the way human beings should live?

Understanding the story of the creation

In the beginning

The Bible assumes that God exists. Everything else has a beginning but God has always existed. He is the creator of the universe. In the beginning nothing had any shape or substance but God's spirit was hovering over this chaos in a protective way, like a bird hovering over its young.

God said …

All God has to do is speak and it happens. For example, he called for light and there was light. The way he gave names to the things he created shows his authority over them. He named the day, the night, the sky, the land and the sea.

Light

Light is a symbol for life and truth in the Bible. Darkness is a symbol of sin and evil. Light is more powerful than darkness. In the New Testament, Jesus called himself the 'light of the world.'

The days

Each day is a unit of time. Some people believe it is an actual day of 24 hours, but most agree that it represents an unspecified period of time and could be millions of years.

Sea creatures

In Old Testament days, the great sea monsters were seen as powerful forces that controlled the world and the people in it. By stating that they were created by God, the writer of Genesis was showing that the Jewish God was more powerful than any other force in the universe. Similarly, the sun and the moon were seen as deities with terrible power. In Genesis they are presented as part of God's planned creation and under his control. They were not to be feared but enjoyed.

God

God is all-powerful. He designed the world and made it out of nothing. He made it so that it would generate itself – he commanded all living things to increase and multiply. He is also a God of order. He made everything in order and he was pleased with each bit he created. The fact that he was pleased with everything shows that it was all good and fit for purpose when he made it. The world could sustain life because it had light and heat from the sun and nutrition from the soil. The universe is beautiful and modern science is constantly discovering new and amazing things about it. He declared that all creation was good and he made human beings to be like him and to carry out his work in the world. On the seventh or '**Sabbath**' day, God 'rested'. He blessed that day and it became the Jewish day of rest to this day.

Essay practice
'God reveals his nature in human beings.' Do you agree? Give reasons for your answer. Show that you have considered more than one point of view.

Humans

We know God values human beings because the story says he made them in his own image. To be in the **image of God** means to be like him in character. For example, human beings have a passion for justice, and they are capable of mercy and love. They are creative and can think and make decisions. God has similar characteristics: he placed humans in a good world and provided them with food and work – looking after his world. They are to have children and bring the world under control; they are to be **responsible rulers** of God's creation and take care of the animals and birds, to make sure the environment is healthy, and they are to care for each other. God provided grain and fruit for food but interestingly there is no mention of meat. Perhaps humans were supposed to be vegetarians ...

justice – treating others fairly

Discuss
Do you have to choose between believing in God and accepting science?

What do you understand? **AO2**

1 Explain what the story of the creation teaches about God.

2 Explain the significance of the words 'In the beginning'.

3 Explain why God was pleased with what he saw.

4 Explain what the story of the creation teaches about God's relationship with the world.

What do you think? **AO3**

5 Why are the commands God gives to human beings important?

6 Do you think that human beings have failed significantly to carry out God's instructions? Give reasons to support your answer.

Essay practice
'No one can answer the question, "Who made the world?"' Do you agree? Give reasons for your answer. Show that you have considered more than one point of view.

Theology in action – science and faith

One of the problems facing Christians today is the way science and faith are often presented in opposition to each other. The rational scientific world is all there is, it is argued. The spiritual world has no place in rational thought because it cannot be observed or tested in a scientific way. On the other hand, as Shakespeare said in his play *Hamlet*, 'There are more things in heaven and earth, Horatio, than are dreamt of in your philosophy.' It is important to understand the limits of science. For example, science cannot deal with purpose or meaning. A moderate Christian view would say that we should not read the Bible as scientific fact. The writer of Genesis expresses the sense of wonder, order and purpose of the universe. Most Christians would say that the Genesis account complements the scientific insight into how matter has evolved from the beginning. The story is timeless and can speak to anyone, no matter where they live or how little education they have received.

Activity

Much research has been done on how the world came into being. Some scientists are Christians and some are atheists. Choose one of the following scientists and research their work:

● Russell Stannard and John Polkinghorne who are Christians

● Stephen Hawking and Richard Dawkins who are atheists

1.2 God and Moses

Starter
Who was Moses?

covenant – an agreement between two people or groups, in this case between God and his people

Discuss
What would it be like to be born a slave? Was Moses right to be so angry about the treatment of one of his people?

This chapter is about how God rescued the Israelites from slavery in Egypt. It is one of the most significant events in the Bible. God chose Moses to bring the Israelites out of slavery in Egypt. In order that he would be able to do this, he was rescued as a baby and brought up in the Egyptian court where he acquired the skills he would need.

Long before the time of Moses, God chose the Israelites to be his people and made a covenant with a man called Abraham, the founder of the Jewish race.

God promised that Abraham would be the father of a great nation and through him all the nations of the world would be blessed. His great grandson was Joseph, of 'amazing technicolour dreamcoat' fame, who was sold into slavery in Egypt, and through a bizarre sequence of events eventually became the Pharaoh's right-hand man.

Famine brought Joseph's father, Jacob, and his family to Egypt and they settled in Goshen, a fertile plain in the Nile estuary. The years passed and the Egyptians forgot why the Israelites were there and resented their prosperity. The Pharaoh of the time, Ramases II, enslaved them and made them work in his labour camps. He also took steps to ensure that they did not grow in number and become a threat, ordering that all baby boys were to be killed at birth.

Into this world **Moses** was born. His mother hid him in a basket in the bulrushes by the River Nile. He was found by the Pharaoh's daughter and brought up as an Egyptian prince. He always knew, however, that he was an Israelite and he was disturbed by the harsh treatment his people received. One day he witnessed one of them being beaten by a slave driver and was so outraged that he killed the Egyptian. Unfortunately, he was seen and had to leave Egypt. He settled in Midian, married the daughter of a priest called Jethro and looked after his sheep. It is at this point that God involved him directly in his rescue plan for his people. Moses emerges as the hero of all three stories in this chapter because he obeyed God and showed great faith and courage in the face of overwhelming odds. He was such a key person in God's plan of salvation that he appeared with Jesus at the Transfiguration (see Chapter 1.4, page 29).

Activity

1 Divide your page into six boxes – three on the left and three on the right. Label the left-hand boxes: The call of Moses; The Passover; Crossing the sea.
2 In each left-hand box write down two questions that you have about each story.
3 Use the three right-hand boxes for your research as you work through the stories.

1.2a The call of Moses: Exodus 3.1–17

Starter

How do you think God talks to people?

◄ '"I am the God of your father, the God of Abraham, the God of Isaac, and the God of Jacob." At this, Moses hid his face, because he was afraid to look at God.' Exodus 3.6.

Read **Exodus 3.1–17.**

What do you know? AO1

1 Outline what happened when Moses saw the burning bush.
2 Describe what God promised Moses at the burning bush.
3 Describe how God called Moses to help the Israelites.

Activity

Write the conversation between God and Moses in play form.

What do you understand? AO2

4 What is this story about?
5 What does the story say about God?

What do you think? AO3

6 Why did God care what happened to the Israelites?

Understanding the story of the burning bush

The burning bush

The flame was a symbol for the presence of God. The bush was not actually burning up so the flame was fuelling itself.

It made Moses curious and attracted him to come closer, where he would then hear God speak.

Fire is also a symbol for purity and holiness.

The Flame

The fire revealed the glory of God.

The revealed character of God

The revealed character of God

God is holy – Moses was asked to take off his shoes in his presence.

God is a living active being – as opposed to the idols of pagan worship which are not alive. The name Yahweh literally means 'being' – I am, I exist.

God is compassionate – he was moved by the suffering of his people.

God honours the covenant he made with his people. He introduced himself as the God of Abraham, Isaac and Jacob, and told Moses about his intention to save his people.

The covenant promise

God was faithful in keeping his covenant with Israel and he outlined what he wanted Moses to do. God showed himself to be a compassionate but all-powerful being, an opponent of injustice and oppression, and a God who intervenes in the world. The promise made to Abraham is reiterated to Moses. God described the land as 'flowing with milk and honey'. The milk would come from sheep and goats, and the honey from bees. Together they would meet the needs of a nomadic nation such as the Israelites.

The land in question was populated by seven tribes but God had promised Abraham that his descendants would conquer their enemies and inhabit their land.

Moses' call

- Moses showed a proper respect for God by removing his shoes and hiding his face.

- He was a very reluctant hero in this story. He kept coming up with reasons why he was not the best person for the job because he didn't want to go back to Egypt and face everything he had left, especially for a task that did not seem likely to be successful.

- He felt inadequate and asked what was so special about him that he should go to the Pharaoh. God's answer required Moses to have faith that he would indeed bring the Israelites out of Egypt to worship on this mountain.

- Moses needed God's authority to lead the Israelites, which is when God revealed his name: 'I AM has sent you'. God's name in Hebrew is Yahweh, which literally means 'being'. His name is a statement that God exists exactly as he existed at the beginning of the world, at the time of Israel's patriarchs, Abraham, Isaac and Jacob. Moses had to have faith to believe that God would be with him too.

What do you understand? **AO2**

1 Explain what this story teaches about the character of God.
2 Explain the part God's covenant with Abraham plays in God's plans.
3 Explain why Moses was so reluctant to do what God asked.
4 Explain what the story teaches about the character of Moses.

What do you think? **AO3**

5 Why might God have chosen a bush that was on fire but not actually burning to communicate with Moses?
6 Why did God choose Moses?

Essay practice
'These days we assume all events must have a rational explanation.' Do you agree? Give reasons for your answer. Show that you have considered more than one point of view.

1.2b The Passover: Exodus 12.1–13

1 The Lord said to Moses and Aaron in Egypt, 2 'This month is to be for you the first month, the first month of your year. 3 Tell the whole community of Israel that on the tenth day of this month each man is to take a lamb for his family, one for each household. 4 If any household is too small for a whole lamb, they must share one with their nearest neighbour, having taken into account the number of people there are. You are to determine the amount of lamb needed in accordance with what each person will eat. 5 The animals you choose must be year-old males without defect, and you may take them from the sheep or the goats. 6 Take care of them until the fourteenth day of the month, when all the people of the community of Israel must slaughter them at twilight. 7 Then they are to take some of the blood and put it on the sides and tops of the doorframes of the houses where they eat the lambs· 8 That same night they are to eat the meat roasted over the fire, along with bitter herbs, and bread made without yeast. 9 Do not eat the meat raw or cooked in water, but roast it over the fire – with the head, legs and internal organs. 10 Do not leave any of it till morning; if some is left till morning, you must burn it. 11 This is how you are to eat it: with your cloak tucked into your belt, your sandals on your feet and your staff in your hand. Eat it in haste; it is the Lord's Passover.

12 'On that same night I will pass through Egypt and strike down every firstborn of both people and animals, and I will bring judgement on all the gods of Egypt. I am the Lord. 13 The blood will be a sign for you on the houses where you are, and when I see the blood, I will pass over you. No destructive plague will touch you when I strike Egypt.'

Exodus 12.1–13

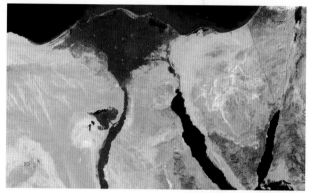

▲ The Nile River Delta, Egypt.

Starter

Do you think people usually get what they deserve for doing wrong?

Discuss

Does God still rescue people caught in bad situations?

What do you know? **AO1**

1 In words or pictures, describe the preparations each family must make for the Passover. Or, imagine you are the member of one such family and write an account of the evening of the Passover.

2 What was going to happen later that night?

What do you understand? **AO2**

3 Why is the event called 'the Passover'?

4 Why must the bread be unleavened (without yeast) and any uneaten lamb burnt?

What do you think? **AO3**

5 What kind of things might make you or your family leave your country for good?

Understanding the story of the Passover

The Passover

God's action in these events was as much a rescue mission as a judgement on Egypt for exploiting and oppressing the Israelites. The **Passover** became a <u>pivotal point</u> in Israel's history because it marked the beginning of their life as a nation under God's protection and guidance.

Jews all over the world celebrate the Passover every year and remember how God rescued them from slavery. They re-enact the meal and tell each other the story of the Passover through the symbols of what they eat. The original Passover would have been very different however because everyone was frightened and insecure, not knowing what was going to happen or whether they would be recaptured by the Egyptians and treated even more harshly. They did not know what it would be like living in the desert or even whether they would survive. They would have had to trust that when Moses told them God would protect and lead them, that he was telling the truth. They were about to experience God's saving action in their lives in a very dramatic way.

The theme of the covenant is developed in the story of the Passover. The Israelites were God's chosen people. He had promised Abraham that he would bless his descendants and give them the cities of their enemies. He had heard their cry for help and, through Moses set about rescuing them.

▲ When Jewish people celebrate the Passover they eat special foods to symbolise parts of the story.

> **Activity**
> Find out about how the Passover is celebrated today.

The significance of the Passover

1 The **new year** was to begin in the spring and not, as previously, in the autumn. It was also a spring festival of new life.

2 A **year-old male lamb without defect** was to be selected. This wasn't any old sheep; this was a valuable male, which did not have anything wrong with it and would, if left, have sired healthy offspring. Only the best would do. There is a connection here for Christians between the sacrifice of the Passover lamb and the sacrifice of Jesus. Jesus is often referred to as the 'Passover lamb'. In Christian tradition, Jesus died to save people from the slavery of sin and death, just as God saved the Israelites from slavery and death at the hands of the Egyptians. The killing of the lamb and the way its blood protected the Israelites, looked forward to the fulfilment of God's plan of salvation for all humanity through Jesus' death.

3 Some of the **blood from the lamb had to be smeared on the lintels and doorposts of the house**. Blood is a symbol for life and played an important part in sacrifices. It is blood that reminds people of God's **covenant** with them. The death of the lamb by the shedding of its blood can be seen as the substitution for the death of the Israelites. When God passed through the land of Egypt, he would see the blood and pass over. The Israelites would escape the judgement of God on Egypt because of the blood. In Christian tradition the blood of Jesus does the same thing – it saves all people from the judgement of God.

4 The lamb was to be **roasted over a fire**. This was the method used by shepherds in the desert. The roasting by fire, the eating of the lamb whole and the burning of any leftovers showed the Israelites' commitment to escape and their faith in God. This was a holy event.

5 They were to eat the lamb with **bitter herbs**. Later the bitter herbs would remind them of their misery as slaves. On this night, they were a symbol of freedom.

6 The **bread** was to be **unleavened**. This means bread made without yeast. The suddenness of the escape meant there was no time for bread to rise before baking. Also, if they were to travel, the bread would keep much longer without yeast in it.

7 The people were to be **ready to travel** as they ate their meal. This meal would not be a relaxed affair; it would be eaten quickly as they waited anxiously for God's anger to fall upon Egypt and the time for their escape.

▲ A year-old male lamb without defect was selected.

▲ The lamb was eaten with bitter herbs.

▲ The bread was unleavened.

▲ The meal was eaten quickly as the people were ready to travel.

What do you understand? **AO2**

1 Explain the importance of the blood on the doorposts and lintels.
2 Explain what was special about the lamb.
3 Why did they have to burn any leftover bits of the roast lamb?
4 How is God's action in this story a sign of his covenant with his people?
5 Explain what this story teaches about God?

What do you think? **AO3**

6 For Christians, what is the link between the Passover and the death of Jesus?
7 Why do you think the Jews continue to celebrate the Passover every year?

Essay practice

'The Passover has no relevance today.' Do you agree? Give reasons for your answer. Show that you have considered more than one point of view.

1.2c Crossing the sea: Exodus 14.10–31

Extract from Moses' diary

Arrived at Pi-Hahiroth – camped here by the sea. Egyptian army very close behind. Will they never give up? Some of the people have started spreading discontent and now there is a huge lobby to go back to Egypt. Honestly, I despair of them with their slave mentality. They're complaining that I have brought them out here deliberately so that they can die – as if there aren't enough coffins in Egypt! 'Didn't you hear us when we specifically told you to leave us alone?' they said. 'Didn't you know that we only wanted to stay and serve the Egyptians?' But no – I had to bring them here, to this place of death. Well, obviously – silly me!

Had a word with them and reminded them that God was with them and not to be afraid. I told them he would rescue them and after today they'd never see an Egyptian again. But I have to confess to being afraid myself when I see the soldiers. Talk about being between a rock and a hard place – or, in our case, a watery place!

Extract from God's diary

Had to give Moses a bit of a shove this evening. There he was, anxiously chewing his nails, standing at the edge of the sea, with the Egyptians closing in. 'Look here,' I said. 'Don't just stand there crying help! Get the Israelites moving.' I knew what he was thinking: where was there to move to? So I told him to lift his walking staff and stretch it out over the sea. I would create a safe passage through the water. Fortunately for the people, he did what I said and I moved the sea – well, I am God after all …

Extract from an Israelite's diary

Now I've seen it all! We've been protected on our journey by a great pillar of cloud, which we followed during the day. Then at night-time with the enemy right behind us, the cloud shifted to be behind us, so the enemy couldn't see us. Nothing occurred during the night but at first light the most incredible thing happened. We were being urged to walk down the beach into the sea and when we got there, there was a long dry passage to the other side – no sea at all, just a wall of water on either side. I admit I was scared as I took the hands of my two children and walked through, but we all came out safely on the opposite bank.

Extract from an Egyptian soldier's last thoughts

Now we've got them! I can just about see them dithering on the banks of the sea. If only it weren't for this blasted cloud that's moved round, we'd be able to attack while they're all arguing about what to do next. It's dawn and the Israelites seem to be on the move. This is truly weird ... they're actually walking through the sea across a great dry stretch of sand. At least we can follow them and take them there. They aren't moving very fast because of all the women and children – Ra rot them! We'll catch them! I urge my horse and chariot between the walls of water. I can feel the sand clogging the wheels and some of the other chariots have lost wheels. All is confusion. I'm going back – the God of the Israelites must be with them ... Oh no! The sea is moving. It's going to sweep us away. I must get back ... Aaaargh!

Extract from God's diary

The people have seen my power and they acknowledge now that I am the one true God. Why didn't they trust me? They must have known I'd protect them. I put a pillar of fire in front of them and a pillar of cloud behind them. I parted the sea for them to cross and I made sure the Egyptians wouldn't trouble them anymore.

Read the whole story in **Exodus 14: 10–31.**

What do you know? AO1

1 What was the reaction of the Israelites when they realised that the Egyptians were coming after them?
2 What was God's advice to Moses?
3 How had God provided protective cover for the Israelites?
4 Describe how the Israelites got to the other side of the sea.
5 What happened to the Egyptians who were chasing them?

What do you understand? AO2

6 What adjectives would you use to describe God from the events in this story?
7 What had Moses done that should have earned the Israelites' trust?

What do you think? AO3

8 What kind of things make us trust someone?

Discuss
What thoughts and emotions might have been running through Moses' mind as he reached the edge of the sea?

Understanding the story of the Exodus

In the story of the **crossing of the sea**, God shows his absolute power through the parting of the sea. He reveals his justice through his judgement of the oppressors, and his love through the constant reassurance he gives his people through Moses.

The word **'exodus'** literally means 'way out' and in this context it refers to the Israelites escaping from Egypt under Moses' leadership. They were to wander round the desert for forty years before entering the Promised Land and during this time they would be shaped into a nation under God – a **theocracy**. The exodus marked the beginning of this physical and spiritual journey. It is seen as conclusive proof of God's love, and justification for his claim on their worship and obedience. Many commands from God are prefixed by the words: 'I am the Lord your God who brought you up out of the land of Egypt'.

God's protection

The pillar of fire showed the Israelites the way forward in the darkness. Fire was symbolic of God's presence so essentially it was God who went before them.

The pillar of cloud hid the Israelites from the pursuing Egyptians. Cloud also denotes God's presence so God was both ahead of and behind them, guiding and defending.

The moaning Israelites

Complaining when you are tired and frightened is a very human trait and the Israelites were both these things. Having run away from slavery in Egypt, they were confronted by a seemingly insurmountable obstacle – the sea. They were hemmed in by the sea, the Egyptian army and the mountain range. Even the miraculous way in which they had been rescued and guided to this point did not prevent them from succumbing to faithless panic and blaming Moses for everything.

God's action

God wanted the people to see that the east wind that drove the seas apart was sent by his command so he told Moses to stretch his hand out over the water. It would also have revived Moses' flagging spirits. It is likely that the Israelites were in the reedy salt marshes at the northern end of the main gulf, where currents and strong winds could temporarily dry out the marshes enough for lightly burdened travellers to cross over quickly. The Hebrew word for 'dry land' is the same as the word used in Genesis 1 when God made the dry land for his creation of the human race. Here the dry land heralds the start of a new creation – the Jewish nation. The 'wall' of water is a poetic metaphor for God's protection against the Egyptians who were trying to circle round them and is not meant to be taken literally. God's leading the Israelites through the Red Sea was a redeeming act, saving them from slavery in Egypt. It can also be seen as a forward look to Jesus' death, which would save people from the slavery of sin, the waters of the sea being the waters of baptism.

The death of the Egyptian army

It was important that the Israelites were left in no doubt as to who had saved them so the defeat of the Pharaoh had to be conclusive. Not only did the Pharaoh change his mind about letting them go but he pursued the Israelites through the desert and across the dangerously boggy salt marshes. When the tide swept back in at God's command, the Egyptians were all killed. The people saw God's power, and their faith was restored in him and in Moses' leadership.

What do you understand? AO2

1 Explain what the story teaches about God.
2 Explain the purpose of the pillar of fire and the pillar of cloud.
3 Explain how God protected the Israelites from the Egyptians.
4 Explain why the Egyptians were so confident of recapturing the Israelites.
5 What was the significance of the 'dry land'?

What do you think? AO3

6 Why is the story of the Exodus so important to the Jews?
7 Should we be concerned with human rights issues in other countries?

Essay practice

'Justice is always worth fighting for.' Do you agree? Give reasons for your answer. Show that you have considered more than one point of view.

Theology in action – humanitarian crisis

Moses rescued the Israelites from slavery in Egypt but they caused political upheaval on their way to the 'Promised Land', problems that are still felt today. People fleeing from a terrible situation are displaced and rootless, and they long for a new identity and a place they can call home. However, it is simply not possible for huge numbers of migrants to settle somewhere without consequences. As the Israelites journeyed to Canaan, they fought anyone who opposed them and overthrew their cities. Today Europe is dealing with a huge refugee crisis with thousands of people fleeing from the horrors of war and ethnic cleansing in the Middle East. These people don't want to conquer their host country but they do pose a serious problem and put social welfare infrastructures under enormous strain. Italy and Greece bear the brunt of this problem but it is an issue for all the countries that refugees move through or settle in. Refugees/asylum seekers experience hardship and prejudice and often struggle to maintain even the most basic of living conditions.

▲ Desperate people use their life's savings to cross the Mediterranean. Many do not survive the journey.

Sami's story

Sami, a 23-year-old Syrian refugee managed to get to Germany where he is trying to put down roots. He has found a job, washing up in a hotel in Berlin. He says they don't teach you at school how to start life from nothing or how to leave everything behind and go to a place where you know no one and can't speak the language. It was a giant leap of faith for Sami. He considers himself blessed to have supportive friends but he worries about his family still in Syria. He says the human spirit pushes you on to believe in a brighter future.

What do you think?　　　　　　　　　　　　AO3

Could you do what Sami did?

Activity

- Find out about the journey taken by a migrant or group of migrants. Map their route and describe the hardships they had to endure. Find out why they had to leave their country.
- Make a poster to promote awareness of the refugee crisis in Europe and make suggestions as to what ordinary people can do to help.

1.3 God and Elijah

Starter

What things make people today turn away from a faith in God?

In this chapter, we meet Elijah and study two stories that show the importance of God's relationship with Israel and with the world. We see how the God who worked miracles through Moses continued to work powerfully through Elijah. In the Old Testament, when God wanted to speak to his people, he did so through a **prophet** and Elijah was one of the greatest prophets. Like Moses, he also appeared with Jesus at his Transfiguration (see page 29).

Elijah lived at a time when the northern kingdom of Israel was ruled by a corrupt king called Ahab and his evil wife Jezebel. She introduced God's people to the worship of the Phoenician god Baal. Baal was the god of rain and fertility and he controlled fire and lightning. She told everyone that it was vital to keep him happy as it was he who made the crops grow and kept the livestock healthy. The people forgot their covenant with God and believed her and worshipped Baal instead of God. As a result, God sent a terrible drought which meant there was no rain for three years.

prophet – a person with a message from God for one or more people

idolatry – the worship of idols

Gentile – anyone who is not a Jew

Idolatry was Israel's most serious sin and for that reason Elijah took drastic action to show Baal to be a false god. It was not really even a contest between two gods, but a contest between God and a delusion.

His challenge to King Ahab meant that everyone would see that it was God who was real and who had the power. It would be a very public and decisive showdown. The faith of the entire nation was at stake, which makes this one of the most significant moments in the Bible.

In the story of Elijah and the widow of Zarephath, God demonstrates that his power and love extend beyond the boundaries of Israel. If the people of Israel will not listen to him, he will turn away from them towards the **Gentiles**. At the same time, he does not forget his covenant with his own people. In the second story of the contest on Mount Carmel, he uses Elijah to show his people that he is the true God and that Baal is a false one without the power to help them. In both stories it is through the prayer of Elijah that God acts. The focus on prayer is key to understanding how God and his people interact.

▲ A stone carving of Baal.

Elijah at Zarephath: 1 Kings 17.8–24

Read **1 Kings 17.8–24**.

Starter
Would you share your last £5 with someone you didn't know?

Summary of the story

- There is widespread famine and drought and everyone is struggling to survive.

- Elijah is told by God to leave Israel where the people have turned to Baal worship, and where there is a price on his head, and to go to Zarephath (Sidon), which is Gentile country.

- There he meets a widow with a young child who, at his request, shares the last of her oil and grain with him.

- Because of her faith, a miracle happens and the oil and grain never run out.

- Then her son tragically dies and she blames herself and Elijah for his death.

- Elijah prays to God and the child is restored to life.

What do you know? `AO1`

1 Imagine you are the widow. Describe your encounter with Elijah on that first day.

2 Outline three ways in which Elijah shows his faith in God in this story.

3 Describe what happened when the boy died.

What do you understand? `AO2`

4 Explain why Elijah went to Zarephath.

5 Explain how this story is about faith – Elijah's as well as the woman's.

What do you think? `AO3`

6 Why did the woman trust Elijah?

Understanding the story of Elijah and the widow of Zarephath

The story about the widow of Zarephath is about two qualities greatly prized by God – **faith** and **obedience**. Elijah had faith that God would protect him even though Zarephath was deep in the heart of Jezebel country. The widow had faith that Elijah's God would somehow provide for her. Both of them obeyed God and put that faith to the test.

When God told Elijah to leave Israel, it was a judgement on Israel because the people had turned away from worshipping him to worshipping Baal. In sending Elijah to the **Gentiles**, God wanted to provoke jealousy and shame in the Jewish nation and to bring about repentance.

The story draws the contrast between Baal, who can't even keep a widow and her son alive in a famine, and God who can, as he brings life with him everywhere he goes. Whether the never-ending supply of oil and grain was supernatural, or neighbours kept her supplied because they were inspired by the widow's generosity in the face of near starvation, is not important. What this story shows is that when people trust God, he is faithful towards them. When people pray to him, he hears and answers.

The death of the widow's son is a shock but the point of the story is threefold:

1 It shows that God is more powerful than death and the uncleanness of death. Under the law, corpses were unclean but notice that Elijah not only touches the dead body of the child, but carries it upstairs and lays himself across it. By doing this he shows that God is stronger than the uncleanness of death.

2 It shows that God hears the prayers of those who have faith and obey him.

3 The woman thought her sins had caught up with her but by raising her son to life, God showed that even sin was no obstacle to him. He reveals himself as the God of new life.

> **Discuss**
> Why are so many stories in the Bible about seemingly insignificant people like this widow?

> Why have you got it in for me, man of God? Did you come to remind me of my sin by killing my son?

What do you know? **AO1**

1 How does the widow show faith in God?
2 How does Elijah demonstrate his faith in God?

What do you understand? **AO2**

3 What does this story teach about the nature of God?
4 What does the story teach about faith?
5 Explain what the story teaches about prayer.

What do you think? **AO3**

6 Why do people pray?

> **Essay practice**
> 'The widow should have saved her last meal for her son rather than giving it to Elijah.' Do you agree? Give reasons for your answer. Show that you have considered more than one point of view.

Elijah at Carmel: 1 Kings 18.19–39

Starter
Should you always stand up for what you think is right, whatever the situation?

Elijah and the prophets of Baal

Read **1 Kings 18.19–29 and 1 Kings 18.30–39.**

Discuss
What does this story show about Baal?

AND GOD ANSWERED.

'O Lord, God of Abraham, Isaac and Israel, let it be known today that you are God in Israel... answer me, O Lord, answer me so that these people will know that you O Lord are God and that you are turning their hearts back again.'

Discuss
What was Elijah's game plan?

Activity
Create a front page for a newspaper describing the events on Mount Carmel.

Understanding the story of the contest on Mount Carmel

The **prophets of Baal** had first go and danced around their altar for hours while Elijah taunted them. They even cut themselves as a symbol of their own self-sacrifice. It was all to no avail.

Elijah wanted the Israelites to be in no doubt of **God's power** so his preparations were an important part of the whole display. He rebuilt the old altar, using twelve stones, which symbolised the twelve tribes of Israel. After the reign of Solomon, his sons had argued over who should be king and they had divided the kingdom so that they could both rule. The twelve stones were a reminder that God was the God of both kingdoms – the ten tribes in the northern kingdom of Israel and the two tribes in the southern kingdom of Judah.

Next Elijah poured **twelve jars of water over the altar.** As there was a terrible drought, this act was one of great faith. He was pouring out what must have been some of the very last water in Israel, like a sacrifice, with the faith that God would send rain once his people returned to worshipping him.

Elijah's prayer to God was simple and totally different from how the priests of Baal had petitioned their god. And the rest is history – God answered Elijah's prayer immediately and sent down such a bolt of fire that it consumed not only the bull, but also the stones and wood and water in the trench round the bottom. There could be no doubt of God's power and authority.

To show repentance and awe in the presence of a mighty king or God, the people knew they had to fall flat on their faces and shout out their allegiance, which is exactly what they did.

Discuss

Why do you think Elijah invited the priests of Baal to go first?

altar – a platform, often made of stones, used for offering sacrifices

worship – giving God reverence, praise and honour

repentance – being truly sorry for something you have done wrong

Activity

Using the information on this page, write an editorial comment on the events you described in your newspaper.

Essay practice

'The twenty-first century has its own "Baals"'. Do you agree? Give reasons for your answer. Show that you have considered more than one point of view.

What do you know? **AO1**

1 Why did Elijah use twelve stones when he built the altar?
2 Why did he pour water over the sacrifice and the altar?
3 Why did the people prostrate themselves at the end of the story?

What do you understand? **AO2**

4 Explain the elaborate preparations Elijah made for his sacrifice.
5 Explain what this story teaches about how God wants his people to live.
6 Explain what the story teaches about God.

What do you think? **AO3**

7 Was Elijah right to put God to the test like this?

Theology in action – religion and politics

In our **pluralist society** (where people from different religious backgrounds live together) we are generally happy for everyone to believe what they want to believe and to worship in their own way as long as it doesn't hurt others. Britain is also becoming more **secular**, with religious faith having less influence in politics and law making. Ethical decisions are not necessarily based on religious ideas or beliefs, although it can be argued that most have their origins in Christianity.

However, the Archbishop of Canterbury, Justin Welby, still speaks out against systems and policies he thinks are unjust or discriminate against the poor and he uses his Christian platform to do so. He believes Christians should be involved in politics. In 2013 he denounced the credit company Wonga as immoral and unjust. Wonga charges very high interest rates and can therefore cause problems for the poor who can end up owing large amounts of money. A debt of £200 for example would incur £70 interest in just one month. On another occasion, in 2016, Welby spoke out against a Brexit deal that only takes economics into consideration and ignores the needs of people.

▲ Archbishop Justin Welby outside 10 Downing Street.

It is easier to go along with the status quo rather than stick your neck out for what you believe. Fear of ridicule, loss of friendship and even the threat of legal action as the result of challenging something on religious grounds, makes people think twice. It was the same in Elijah's day with a powerful and vindictive king and queen telling the Jews to bow down to Baal, and killing them if they worshipped God. Elijah often went through agonies of fear but he always obeyed God in the end and God did not let him down. People often need signs before they'll change the way they think and on this occasion God gave them one and they turned away from Baal and back to him.

Discuss
Should religion have a place in politics?

Activity
1 What does it mean to live in a 'pluralist society'?
2 Describe one way in which the Archbishop of Canterbury has spoken out about what he believes to be wrong.
3 If Elijah were alive today, what might he speak out against?

1.4 God, Moses, Elijah and Jesus

The Transfiguration took place shortly after Peter had declared Jesus to be the Messiah, or Christ as it is in Greek. The disciples' recognition of him had led Jesus to tell them that he would suffer and die but then be raised to life again. The Transfiguration teaches about Jesus' divine identity as God's son. God is present with him uniquely and unites his past actions in the world with those of the present and the future. The presence of **Moses** the lawgiver and **Elijah** the prophet from the Old Testament endorse who Jesus is and he is ranked alongside them as being the fulfilment of law and prophecy. Their presence urged the disciples to listen to Jesus when he talked about his approaching death. The change in Jesus' appearance looked forward to his resurrection and ascension when he would take his rightful place with God in heaven.

Starter
Does it matter what we believe about Jesus?

The Transfiguration: Mark 9.2–13

2 After six days Jesus took Peter, James and John with him and led them up a high mountain, where they were all alone. There he was transfigured before them. 3 His clothes became dazzling white, whiter than anyone in the world could bleach them. 4 And there appeared before them Elijah and Moses, who were talking with Jesus. 5 Peter said to Jesus, 'Rabbi, it is good for us to be here. Let us put up three shelters – one for you, one for Moses and one for Elijah.' 6 (He did not know what to say, they were so frightened.) 7 Then a cloud appeared and enveloped them, and a voice came from the cloud: 'This is my Son, whom I love. Listen to him!' 8 Suddenly, when they looked around, they no longer saw anyone with them except Jesus. 9 As they were coming down the mountain, Jesus gave them orders not to tell anyone what they had seen until the Son of Man had risen from the dead. 10 They kept the matter to themselves, discussing what 'rising from the dead' meant. 11 And they asked him, 'Why do the teachers of the law say that Elijah must come first?' 12 Jesus replied, 'To be sure, Elijah does come first, and restores all things. Why then is it written that the Son of Man must suffer much and be rejected? 13 But I tell you, Elijah has come, and they have done to him everything they wished, just as it is written about him.'

Mark 9.2–13

▲ *The Transfiguration* by Carl Bloch.

Activity
Imagine you are Peter. Write your diary entry for the day of the Transfiguration.

Understanding the story of the Transfiguration

The Transfiguration probably took place on Mount Hermon, giving Jesus the necessary privacy from the crowds. Mountain tops are also seen as holy places. A week earlier, Peter had made his famous declaration of faith – that he thought Jesus was the long awaited Messiah, and now he, James and John, Jesus' closest disciples, were to experience Jesus clothed in God's glory. The word **Transfiguration** means change of appearance and the account says Jesus' clothes became dazzling white. The disciples still didn't understand who Jesus really was so they were afraid.

Moses and Elijah

The appearance of Moses and Elijah is very significant because they represented two important traditions in the Old Testament – the law and the prophets.

Moses represented the **law** because it was he who received the law on Mount Sinai from God himself. The commandments were the only way the Jewish people had of knowing how God wanted them to live. Moses was a great hero who merits the title 'Messiah' because he rescued the Jews from slavery in Egypt.

Elijah represented the **Jewish prophets**, through whom God communicated with his people. Elijah was the most important of the prophets. Jews also believed that he would appear before the coming of the Messiah. In their conversation coming down from the mountain, Jesus told his disciples that Elijah had already come. Jesus would almost certainly have been referring to John the Baptist who told everyone who Jesus was when Jesus was baptised by him in the River Jordan.

▲ A Sukkah is a temporary structure where meals are eaten for the week during the festival, Sukkot.

Peter's suggestion

The suggestion to build shelters for Jesus, Moses and Elijah seems to be a very peculiar thing for Peter to say, but the idea has its roots in the Old Testament. Before the Temple was built the Israelites kept the sacred Ark of the Covenant in a special tent called the 'Tabernacle'. They believed that God's presence rested within the Tabernacle so when Peter saw Jesus, Moses and Elijah wrapped in God's glory, he thought tents were what was needed. Sukkot, the Jewish festival of tabernacles, specifically remembers this period of Jewish history and people make shelters to remind them of the time God guided and protected them in the desert after the Exodus.

Peter's suggestion also shows that he has partially understood what was going on. The Jews believed that one day God would reveal himself fully and everyone would live in tents. However, in the event, no notice was taken of Peter, who was left feeling rather foolish, when a cloud hid Moses, Elijah and Jesus from his sight.

The cloud

The cloud is a symbol of God's presence. In the Exodus a pillar of cloud led the Israelites out of Egypt. A cloud had come down at Jesus' baptism and as on that day, a voice spoke from the cloud. God told the disciples that Jesus was his Son, whom he loved and that they were to listen to him.

The conversation on the way down the mountain

What the disciples had been told would only properly make sense after the Resurrection. This was why Jesus told them not speak of what they had seen until then. It is clear from the disciples' complete amazement after the Resurrection that they had not understood what Jesus meant. They thought he was talking about the Resurrection at the end of the world, not Jesus himself rising from the dead in the near future.

The Son of Man

This is the term Jesus used most often to describe himself. It is an Old Testament title and in using it, Jesus was identifying himself with human suffering. He was the perfect example of how God's will can be carried out by human beings in this world. By using it on this occasion he was saying that his path was that of suffering and death, not worldly glory and fame, but the disciples missed the point.

What do you understand? **AO2**

1 Why did Jesus' appearance become 'dazzling white'?
2 Explain the presence of Moses and Elijah at the Transfiguration.
3 Explain the significance of the cloud.
4 Why did Peter suggest building three shelters/tents?
5 Explain what the term 'Son of Man' means.
6 Explain what the story teaches about Jesus.
7 What does the Transfiguration reveal about Jesus' mission?

What do you think? **AO3**

8 What emotions do you think Jesus might have experienced? Give reasons to support your answer.

Essay practice

'Jesus was more than just a teacher.' Do you agree? Give reasons for your answer. Show that you have considered more than one point of view.

1.5 Jesus' miracles

Starter

Why did Jesus perform miracles?

Discuss

Do you think people's illnesses are ever caused by sin?

In this chapter, we look at three miracles: healing a paralysed man, calming a storm and feeding five thousand people. For many Christians, Jesus' miracles make a statement about who he was. Only God is powerful enough to do all these things with a single word of command. If Jesus has this power, he must be divine. The miracles tell us about God's plan of salvation through Jesus. In John's gospel they are called signs because they point to Jesus' divine nature. The miracles of Jesus fulfil the Old Testament hope of a Messiah and they are examples of how God acts in the world.

1.5a The paralysed man: Mark 2.1–12

Read **Mark 2.1–12**.

What do you know?　　　　　　　　　　　**AO1**

1　How did the friends show their persistence?
2　Why did the scribes criticise Jesus?
3　How did Jesus answer them?

Flow charts are a good way to summarise a story

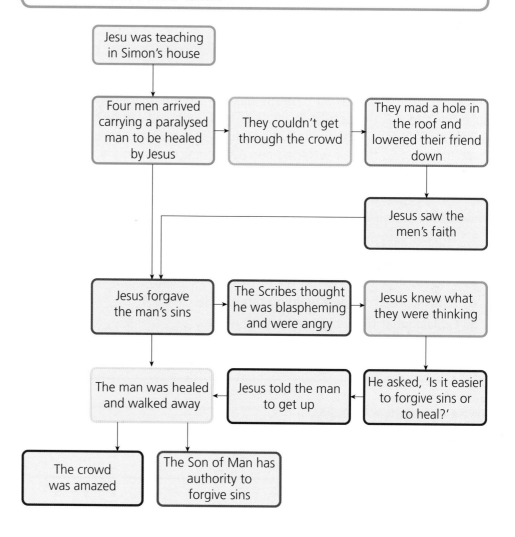

Jesu was teaching in Simon's house

↓

Four men arrived carrying a paralysed man to be healed by Jesus → They couldn't get through the crowd → They mad a hole in the roof and lowered their friend down

↓

Jesus saw the men's faith

↓

Jesus forgave the man's sins → The Scribes thought he was blaspheming and were angry → Jesus knew what they were thinking

↓

The man was healed and walked away ← Jesus told the man to get up ← He asked, 'Is it easier to forgive sins or to heal?'

↓

The crowd was amazed　　The Son of Man has authority to forgive sins

Understanding the story of the paralysed man

The **miracles** of Jesus need to be seen in the light of his divine power and in his purpose in the world, which is salvation.

miracle – a happening that cannot be fully explained by natural events or human reason

Jesus heals the paralysed man

This is a dramatic story and one which raises several interesting points.

- It was the faith of the four friends rather than that of the man himself that led to his being healed. Faith is having an active trust in someone or something. Nearly all the other healing miracles required the faith of the person needing healing.

- Jesus' first action was to forgive the man for his sin. Christians believe that sin is something that cuts people off from God. It can be a wrong attitude as well as bad actions or words. By forgiving the man's sins, Jesus showed his care for people's spiritual health as well as their physical well-being.

- Jesus caused an angry reaction from the **Scribes**. They followed Jesus around on purpose to try and catch him out. Popularity was regarded with suspicion and fear – 'Who is this man? What is his authority? He's not one of us …'. The Scribes believed that only God could forgive sins, so when Jesus forgave the man, they said it was **blasphemy**. Jesus' action marked the beginning of the conflict between himself and the religious authorities.

▲ Jesus the healer.

- Jesus' reply to the Scribes' question proved his authority to forgive sins because he told the man to get up and walk, which the man did. If, as most people believed, God had sent his paralysis as a punishment, God must have forgiven him if he could now walk.

- The Old Testament prophecies about the Messiah said that the lame would walk, the blind would see and the dumb would speak. Thus Jesus curing the paralysed man was a sign that he was the promised Messiah.

blasphemy – speaking against God or making yourself equal to God

What do you understand? **AO2**

1 Explain the part faith played in this story.
2 Explain why the Scribes were angry with Jesus.
3 What did Jesus show about himself by forgiving the man's sins and healing him?
4 What was behind the concern shown by the Scribes?
5 Why do you think Jesus forgave the man's sins before healing him?

What do you think? **AO3**

6 Is physical health more important than spiritual well-being?

1.5b The calming of the storm: Mark 4.35–41

Starter

What would be your first reaction if you witnessed an extraordinary event such as this one?

35 That day when evening came, he said to his disciples, 'Let us go over to the other side.' 36 Leaving the crowd behind, they took him along, just as he was, in the boat. There were also other boats with him. 37 A furious squall came up, and the waves broke over the boat, so that it was nearly swamped. 38 Jesus was in the stern, sleeping on a cushion. The disciples woke him and said to him, 'Teacher, don't you care if we drown?'

39 He got up, rebuked the wind and said to the waves, 'Quiet! Be still!' Then the wind died down and it was completely calm.

40 He said to his disciples, 'Why are you so afraid? Do you still have no faith?'

41 They were terrified and asked each other, 'Who is this? Even the wind and the waves obey him!'

Mark 4.35–41

◀ *Jesus calming the storm* by He Qi.

What do you know?　AO1

1　Describe what happened when Jesus took the disciples out in the boat.
2　When the disciples woke Jesus, what did they expect him to do?
3　What was the disciples' reaction once everything had calmed down?

What do you understand?　AO2

4　Explain why Jesus questioned the disciples' faith?
5　What does this story reveal about who Jesus is?

Activity

You are a reporter with the *Galilee Gazette*. Interview one of the disciples on the boat about what happened. Add pictures and choose a dramatic title for your article.

Understanding the story of the calming of the storm

Discuss

Why did Jesus perform this miracle?

Jesus challenged the disciples' lack of faith. They had witnessed him performing incredible miracles like healing the paralysed man and now they were a mass of quivering jelly in the face of a storm. This miracle left the disciples questioning who Jesus was since he had the power to calm a storm.

If you had been a Jew living in first-century Israel, you would have had a very healthy respect for the sea. You would have grown up with the belief that evil spirits lived in the sea and in the deep waters under the earth. If you earned your living by fishing, you would also have experienced sudden squalls and know how easily your boat could be capsized. A rough sea was a terrifying thing. You would have believed that the spirits were coming up to the surface and attacking you, and at any moment you could be thrown into the water and drown. This story therefore is about more than Jesus' authority over nature; it is about his authority over the spirit world too. His instruction 'Be still!' is similar to the way he speaks when casting out evil spirits.

Going out in a boat is always risky, but such was Jesus' trust in God, he was able to sleep peacefully, even through a storm. Mark adds the detail that he was asleep in the back of the boat. This shows both Jesus' humanity – he was exhausted so he slept – and his deity – the wind and the waves obeyed him.

You can also see this story as a message of peace to the persecuted Church of the first century. The stormy waves are a symbol for the troubles the Church was experiencing when Mark was writing his gospel. The disciples were frightened of the storm and indignant that Jesus should sleep through the danger. They needed to be reminded, just as the early Christians did, that Jesus was both with them and in control, and that they should have faith through their difficulties. The resulting calm after the storm represents the true peace that God's triumph over evil brings.

What do you understand? **AO2**

1 Why were people afraid of the sea at the time of Jesus?

2 What does the story teach about Jesus? Give evidence from the passage for each observation.

3 What does the story teach about the disciples?

4 How might this story have helped the early Christians who read it?

5 What does this story teach about faith?

6 Explain what Jesus expected of his disciples.

1.5c The feeding of the five thousand: Mark 6.30–44

35 By this time it was late in the day, so his disciples came to him. 'This is a remote place,' they said, 'and it's already very late. 36 Send the people away so that they can go to the surrounding countryside and villages and buy themselves something to eat.'

37 But he answered, 'You give them something to eat.' They said to him, 'That would take more than half a year's wages! Are we to go and spend that much on bread and give it to them to eat?'

38 'How many loaves do you have?' he asked. 'Go and see.' When they found out, they said, 'Five – and two fish.'

39 Then Jesus directed them to have all the people sit down in groups on the green grass. 40 So they sat down in groups of hundreds and fifties. 41 Taking the five loaves and the two fish and looking up to heaven, he gave thanks and broke the loaves. Then he gave them to his disciples to distribute to the people. He also divided the two fish among them all. 42 They all ate and were satisfied, 43 and the disciples picked up twelve basketfuls of broken pieces of bread and fish. 44 The number of men who had eaten was five thousand.

Mark 6.35–44

What do you know?　　AO1

1 Describe what happened after the disciples told Jesus how much fish and bread they had.
2 What was the disciples' objection to Jesus' suggestion that they feed the crowd themselves?
3 Imagine you were one of the crowd when this miracle happened. Write about the experience.

What do you think?　　AO3

4 Was there anything in Jesus' actions that suggested he was performing a miracle? Give a reason for your answer.

Understanding the story of the feeding of the five thousand

This miracle is important because it is the only one recorded in all four gospels. It reads like an eyewitness account, probably Peter's, as his memories are what mostly make up Mark's gospel:

- The green grass – it must have been late spring.

- The time of day – it was sunset, so about 6 p.m.

- The 'groups' people sat down in – the word used actually means rows, so in Peter's memory the crowd must have sat in orderly rows.

- The twelve baskets – every orthodox Jew carried a basket, mainly used to hold kosher food. The twelve baskets full of scraps at the end almost certainly belonged to the twelve disciples who had collected everything so that nothing should be wasted. They also show God's abundance; that he provided more than enough for everyone's need.

The story shows **two reactions to peoples' need**:

- The disciples: these people are tired and hungry; send them away to make their own arrangements.

- Jesus: these people are tired and hungry; give them something to eat.

The story shows **two reactions to human resources**:

- The disciples said what they had couldn't possibly make any difference. A denarius was worth about 3½ pence and was the standard day's wage for the working man. Even if they worked solidly for six months, the disciples couldn't pay for everyone.

- Jesus' response was to ask how much they had, which was five loaves and two small fish. Barley loaves were the food of the very poor, being coarse and cheap. The salt-fish would have been the size of sardines. The disciples needed to learn that with Jesus anything was possible – to use what they had and trust God to do the rest. This experience would help them later when they were faced with difficult situations and felt inadequate and afraid.

So, what actually happened?

There are two main theories. Some people say that when people saw the boy sharing his humble meal, they all took out what they had and followed his example. It was a miracle that took place in people's hearts. The crowd would have included some wealthy men and women whose instinct would not normally have been to share their food with people they did not know. The poor similarly might have been reluctant to share the little they had. That everyone did share would have been a miracle in itself.

Others say that in Jesus' hands, the fish and the bread miraculously did not run out until every last person had had enough. This was evidence that Jesus had divine power and, along with his other miracles, gave authority to everything he said and did.

What do you understand?

AO2

1 What things suggest that this was an eye-witness account?

2 Explain why there were twelve baskets of food left over.

3 Why do you think Jesus asked his disciples to feed the people?

4 Suggest two possible explanations of what happened.

5 Explain the disciples' objection to Jesus' suggestion that they should feed the people?

Theology in action – modern miracles

Miracles cannot be repeated so it is very difficult to examine them scientifically. It is almost impossible to disprove them or make any scientific statement about them. For example, you cannot order a miraculous healing so that you can observe it. Science can say how things usually behave and do not behave, so it can make general statements about miracles, but such statements neither prove nor disprove them.

Whatever may or may not have happened in Jesus' day, people still claim to have witnessed miracles in this day and age and interpret narrow escapes such as the Hudson River landing, as miraculous.

▲ Passengers step out of the aircraft onto the wings of Flight 1549.

The Hudson River crash

On 16 January 2009, the US Airways Airbus A320 crash landed in the Hudson River just minutes after take off. The pilot, Captain Chesley Sullenberger, managed to ditch the plane after its engines were disabled by a flock of geese, without any loss of life. There were no boats in its path and as soon as it landed several water taxis rushed to help. All 155 passengers and crew, including a baby, were safely evacuated before the aircraft sank. The only significant injury was to someone who broke both legs.

As the aeroplane came in low over the river and it became clear they were going to crash, many people on board started praying. One of the passengers Jeff Kolodjay. said that he heard a loud bang and the plane filled with smoke. 'It was pretty scary, man. We got out by the luck of God. I take my hat off to the pilot.' The Governor of New York State called it the 'Miracle on the Hudson'.

Healing centres

Lourdes

The shrine at Lourdes in France is one of the most famous healing centres in the world and thousands flock there hoping to be cured. While they are there they receive the laying on of hands, prayer and counselling. Healing is occasionally physical but many more people experience emotional and spiritual healing. This kind of healing goes deeper, restoring the spirit into wholeness. Healing can occur without there being a cure for a person's physical condition.

▲ Pilgrims gather under the statue of the Virgin Mary at Lourdes, France.

Essay practice

1 'There is more than one kind of healing.' Do you agree? Give reasons for your answer. Show that you have considered more than one point of view.

2 'Sceptics have a valid point.' Do you agree? Give reasons for your answer. Show that you have considered more than one point of view.

NB: Sceptics in this context are people who believe we should seek rational explanations for apparently miraculous events.

Activity

1 Why did the State Governor call the rescue of Flight 1549 a miracle?

2 Why did the passengers on the aircraft start praying?

3 What is offered at Lourdes that makes people go there?

4 Do services of healing fulfil a useful purpose? Give reasons to support your answer.

1.6 Jesus' mission

In this last chapter in Topic 1, we will read about the climax of the story of God's plan of salvation that runs through the Bible, and see the true nature of God's relationship with the world. John's gospel says this: 'For God so loved the world that he gave his one and only Son, that whoever believes in him shall not perish but have eternal life' (John 3.16). Central to the Christian faith is the belief that all people sin and are in need of saving from the penalty of sin, which is death. This was Jesus' mission – to die and pay that penalty in their place. But that was not the last word because God raised Jesus from the dead thus defeating death and fulfilling his long-term plan for the world. In the Resurrection, Jesus' divinity is validated.

Starter
Under what circumstances might a person be prepared to give up their life for someone else?

The crucifixion: Mark 15.22–39

22 They brought Jesus to the place called Golgotha (which means 'the place of the skull'). 23 Then they offered him wine mixed with myrrh, but he did not take it. 24 And they crucified him. Dividing up his clothes, they cast lots to see what each would get.

25 It was nine in the morning when they crucified him. 26 The written notice of the charge against him read: the king of the Jews. 27 They crucified two rebels with him, one on his right and one on his left.

29 Those who passed by hurled insults at him, shaking their heads and saying, 'So! You who are going to destroy the temple and build it in three days, 30 come down and save yourself!'

31 In the same way the chief priests and the teachers of the law mocked him among themselves. 'He saved others,' they said, 'but he can't save himself! 32 Let this Messiah, this King of Israel, come down now from the cross, that we may see and believe.' Those crucified with him also heaped insults on him.

33 At noon, darkness came over the whole land until the ninth hour. 34 And at three in the afternoon Jesus cried out in a loud voice, '*Eloi, Eloi, lama sabachthani?*' – which means, 'My God, my God, why have you forsaken me?'.

35 When some of those listening near heard this, they said, 'Listen, he's calling Elijah.'

36 Someone ran, filled a sponge with wine vinegar, put it on a staff, and offered it to Jesus to drink. 'Now leave him alone. Let's see if Elijah comes to take him down,' he said.

37 With a loud cry, Jesus breathed his last.

38 The curtain of the temple was torn in two from top to bottom. 39 And when the centurion, who stood there in front of Jesus, heard his cry and saw how he died, he said, 'Surely this man was the Son of God!'

Mark 15.22–39

Activity
Discuss what Jesus' death means to Christians today. Then make a large cross out of paper and depict those ideas, using clips from magazines, drawings, words – anything you like.

What do you know? **AO1**

1 List the actions of the Roman soldiers in this story.
2 What were the various reactions of people who saw Jesus hanging on the cross?
3 Describe what happened at noon.
4 What happened at three in the afternoon?

What do you understand? **AO2**

5 Why might the insults hurled at Jesus have been almost worse than his physical pain?

Understanding the story of the crucifixion

Background to the story

Pilate was the Roman governor of Israel and he was the only person in the country who could condemn a man to death. This was why the Jewish leaders had to invent some charges and bring Jesus before him. They wanted Jesus dead for the following reasons:

- He was too popular. Everywhere he went, he attracted people – an enormous crowd welcomed Jesus into Jerusalem for the Passover festival.

- He threatened their authority and was outspoken against them.

- He made himself equal to God, which to them was blasphemy.

Under Roman law the charges were as follows:

- He was leading the Jewish nation's loyalty away from Rome.

- He had forbidden taxes to be paid to Rome – the usual accusation against Zealots (resistance fighters).

- Jesus had claimed the title 'king', which was a treasonable offence.

▲ The long nails and the crown of thorns are deeply symbolic of Jesus' crucifixion.

Golgotha

Golgotha was the place of execution outside the city of Jerusalem. A group of women always went to crucifixions to offer some pain relief but Jesus refused it. Everyone who walked past insulted him and mocked his claim to destroy the temple and rebuild it in three days. They thought he was referring to the huge stone temple in Jerusalem that had been built after the exile 400 years before. Jesus had been talking about the temple of his body, which would be 'rebuilt' in three days when he rose from the dead. They challenged him by saying they would believe his claims if he came down from the cross.

However, right at the beginning of his ministry Jesus had spent forty days in the desert being tempted by the devil. One of the temptations had been to perform a superhero stunt and prove beyond doubt that he was God. He was not about to give in. The presence of the chief priests and the teachers of the law was supposed to show everyone that this Jesus was a pretend Messiah and therefore deserved everything he got.

At the sixth hour, the sky went dark. This was deeply symbolic of the light of the world (Jesus) being extinguished (dying).

Jesus' words from Psalm 22 are in Aramaic and 'Eloi' sounds like the word 'Elijah'. Those who witnessed the execution thought he was calling on Elijah to rescue him. Christians believe that in that moment Jesus was taking on himself the punishment for the sins of the human race. This separated him from God and therefore caused his anguish.

Two significant things happened at the moment of Jesus' death:

- The curtain dividing the Holy of Holies from the rest of the Temple was ripped in two. God was believed to be present in a very special way in the Holy of Holies and so Christians see this as a symbol of Jesus' death removing the barrier between God and humans. The Holy of Holies was a separate area believed to contain God's presence in a special way. It was so holy that only the High Priest could enter it once a year and only after the offering of a special sacrifice. Christians see the ripping of the curtain as a sign from God that he had accepted the atoning sacrifice of Jesus' death. God's relationship with his creation was restored.

- A hard-bitten soldier who was a complete stranger to Jesus made a tribute to him by saying that he must have been the Son of God. He probably meant that Jesus had been a very great man, even godlike.

Jesus died at three o'clock on the Friday afternoon. As the Sabbath began at six o'clock, there were only three hours left to take him down from the cross and bury him.

God's plan of salvation

Christians believe that God had a plan right from the beginning to save the world from the consequences of its sin. Old Testament prophets spoke of this plan. Here is an extract from one of them, a man called Isaiah:

> 3 'He was despised and rejected by mankind, a man of suffering, and familiar with pain. ... 5 he was pierced for our transgressions, he was crushed for our iniquities; the punishment that brought us peace was on him, and by his wounds we are healed. ... 12 For he bore the sin of many, and made intercession for the transgressors [spoke up on behalf of those who did wrong].'
>
> *Isaiah 53.3–12*

Jesus gave his life as a **sacrifice** for human sin. The Old Testament helps explain this because in the ritual of sacrifice, God accepted the life of the animal as an atonement for the sins of the people. These sacrifices had to be offered every year. Jesus' sacrifice was once and for all. Jesus' death removed the barrier of sin, allowing humans direct access to God.

Discuss

Look at the prophecy from Isaiah. How might it link with Jesus' death?

---

atonement – getting back into a good relationship with God – 'at-one-ment'. It means being forgiven by him

---

What do you think? AO3

7 Is it better for an innocent person to die if it means thousands of people can live?

Essay practice

'Jesus did not need to die.' Do you agree? Give reasons for your answer. Show that you have considered more than one point of view.

What do you understand? AO2

1 Explain why the Jewish leaders wanted Jesus dead.

2 Why did people taunt him when he was on the cross?

3 Explain the words Jesus spoke just before he died.

4 Explain what was significant about what happened at the moment of his death.

5 Why might it be appropriate that Jesus died between two obviously bad men?

6 Explain how Jesus' death could be seen as a sacrifice.

The Resurrection: John 20.24–9

Starter
Is scepticism always a good thing?

24 Now Thomas (also known as Didymus), one of the Twelve, was not with the disciples when Jesus came. 25 So the other disciples told him, 'We have seen the Lord!' But he said to them, 'Unless I see the nail marks in his hands and put my finger where the nails were, and put my hand into his side, I will not believe.'

26 A week later his disciples were in the house again, and Thomas was with them. Though the doors were locked, Jesus came and stood among them and said, 'Peace be with you!'

27 Then he said to Thomas, 'Put your finger here; see my hands. Reach out your hand and put it into my side. Stop doubting and believe.'

28 Thomas said to him, 'My Lord and my God!'

29 Then Jesus told him, 'Because you have seen me, you have believed; blessed are those who have not seen and yet have believed.'

John 20.24–9

What do you know? AO1

1 Describe what happened when the disciples told Thomas they had seen Jesus.

2 Describe the conversation between Thomas and Jesus the following week.

What do you understand? AO2

3 Why didn't Thomas accept the disciples' word that Jesus had risen from the dead?

4 What evidence is there in the story that Jesus' body was different after the Resurrection?

5 To whom do you think Jesus was referring when he said, 'Blessed are those who have not seen and yet have believed.'

Activity

Using the short conversation in John's gospel as a starting point, write a dialogue between one of the disciples who had seen Jesus, and Thomas who hadn't. What was Thomas really thinking? Why didn't he believe his friends? What arguments could the other disciples use?

Understanding the story of the Resurrection

Discuss

Why does an eye-witness account carry more authority than a second-hand one?

Doubting Thomas

Thomas was called 'Doubting Thomas' because he did not believe his friends when they said they had seen Jesus and he was alive. We don't know why Thomas wasn't with the disciples immediately after Jesus' crucifixion. He clearly felt uncomfortable about accepting their word, because people don't just come back from the dead. He refused to believe without seeing for himself, even to the point of touching Jesus' wounds. His scepticism has helped thousands of Christians cope with their own doubt. Jesus himself was not unsympathetic towards him.

> I won't believe you unless I see for myself.

Jesus gives Thomas the proof

Thomas had to wait a week before he had the proof he wanted. Notice that the Bible says the doors were locked when Jesus appeared a second time. This implies that his 'resurrection body', although recognisable, was different and that he could appear and disappear at will. His greeting was the traditional one of peace, 'Shalom'. There was no need to be afraid. As he had done with the other disciples a week earlier, he showed Thomas his hands and his side, which had a gaping wound from the spear that was thrust into it.

Jesus used the same words to Thomas as Thomas had used to the disciples. This must have made quite an impression on him as Jesus hadn't been there to hear them. When Jesus told him to stop doubting and believe, Thomas had already done so as his words to Jesus confirm.

Thomas' declaration of faith is why John includes this story. He didn't just say, 'Oh hi, Jesus – it really is you then!' He made a statement of faith. Thomas recognised that Jesus was divine. Only if he were God could he have risen from the dead. Only if he had divine power could he have known what Thomas had said to the disciples. Everything he had seen and learnt over the course of Jesus' ministry suddenly made sense. His statement demonstrated the shift in the disciples' thinking to accept that the risen Jesus was God.

> My Lord and my God!

Future believers

Jesus commends future generations who hear about him – his death and resurrection, his words and actions – and believe even without the benefit of seeing for themselves. Their faith will rest on the reports of others. Jesus said such faith is nobler than Thomas' faith. It is the faith that would see the Christian Church through times of persecution and secular challenges. This is true faith.

The evidence for the Resurrection

The Christian faith is centred round the belief that Jesus rose from the dead. The early Christians firmly believed in the bodily resurrection. The stories of the appearances of Jesus after his resurrection, like this one in John's gospel, are there as evidence of what they had seen. So let us examine what evidence there is.

1 The disciples were turned from a frightened group, who had just seen their leader crucified, into a strong courageous band who told everyone that Jesus was alive. They were prepared to preach the Resurrection and to die for that belief. This sudden transformation is undisputed.

2 The early Church put belief in the Resurrection into their creed.

3 St Paul, one of the Apostles and early missionaries, did a study of the evidence. He said that Jesus had appeared to five hundred people at the same time as well as individually to the disciples and some women. Most would have still been alive when Paul was carrying out his study and it is reasonable to assume that some had spoken to Paul. Jesus had also appeared in a special way to Paul.

4 The Gospels all contain stories of Jesus appearing to his disciples, both collectively and individually.

5 The Gospels all include evidence of an empty grave. If there had been a body, the Romans and the Jewish religious leaders would surely have found it as it was in their interests to put an end to the rumours that Jesus was alive.

6 The stories are written simply and do not contain any symbolism that needs special decoding or understanding.

Another way of understanding the Resurrection

Some Christians say that the important thing about the Resurrection is not the physical body, but the spiritual one. Even if the accounts of the Resurrection appearances were written to reveal the truth in a way that made it easy to understand, what matters is that Jesus is present in people's lives and can help them to live a holy life just as he was there for his disciples and the early Christians.

What do you know? **AO1**

1 Describe two different ways of understanding the Resurrection.
2 What evidence is there that the Resurrection took place?

What do you understand? **AO2**

3 Why is Thomas called 'Doubting Thomas'?
4 Why do you think he needed proof of what the other disciples had seen?
5 Explain why Jesus said people who had believed without seeing would be the more blessed.
6 Explain the significance of Thomas saying, 'My Lord and my God!'.

What do you think? **AO3**

7 Do you think that doubting is the first step towards belief? Give reasons to support your answer.

> **Discuss**
>
> Read page 127 of Section 2 and discuss what people believe about life after death. How does the Christian view differ from the other views?

> **Essay practice**
>
> 'If Jesus had not risen from the dead there would be no Christian faith today.' Do you agree? Give reasons for your answer. Show that you have considered more than one point of view.

Theology in action – who was Jesus really?

The disciples witnessed a series of very significant events but it was only after the Resurrection that the things Jesus had done during his life, what he had said and the way he had died, began to make sense. They realised that Jesus not only had divine power and authority but that he himself was divine. However, this was a realisation that came through faith and that continues to be the case today. People are still not sure who Jesus was and many books have been written on the subject. Here are some common viewpoints on Jesus that you might hear.

'Jesus was the Son of God'

Christians believe that Jesus was the Son of God. They claim he came into the world especially to die so that sin could be forgiven and everyone could be made right with God. They believe that God raised Jesus from the dead, which proves he is God. Christians say that the evidence for the resurrection is the sort of evidence accepted every day in law courts – in other words, the evidence of eye witnesses. Many people said they saw Jesus.

On the other hand, people argue that there is no proof as to who Jesus was. They say that if Jesus is dead, he can't be God. They say the other opinions about who Jesus was are more plausible.

'Jesus was a prophet'

Others claim that Jesus was a prophet. He was a good and wise man who helped people. He set a good example, stood up for outcasts and stood up against injustice and cruelty. He condemned religious leaders for their hypocrisy and he preached a message of love and forgiveness. They say that there is a lot of symbolism in what Jesus said and that he had an extraordinary understanding of God. His example, rather than what he said about himself, is what inspires people today.

On the other hand, Jesus made a lot of strange claims for a 'good man'. He said he had power over death and disease, and he forgave people their sins. He also told people they could be saved by believing in him. If he was only a man, then he is long dead and can't save anybody. It can be argued that giving people false hope is not the action of a good man.

'Jesus is a myth'

Some people claim that Jesus never really existed, or if he did he certainly was nothing like the Jesus portrayed by the church. They say stories about Jesus have been exaggerated over the centuries to fit in with what people believed.

On the other hand, there is evidence that Jesus was a real person. He is mentioned by early historians like Josephus. The first Christians must have been thoroughly convinced about who Jesus was if they were prepared to die for their beliefs. In the days before history came to be written down as it is today, people passed on events through telling stories and these were usually fairly reliable. The first stories about Jesus were written only forty years after his death.

So, what now?

If we were to hold the view that Jesus is a myth, then we would not build our lives on his spiritual teaching, although we might follow his moral guidelines. A good many Christians might say there are mythical elements to the Jesus of the Gospels but these myths hold important truths. However, it would mean that Jesus had no real relevance to anyone's life today.

If we were to hold the view that Jesus was a good man, we would be likely to try to live a good life according to his teaching. We might believe that Jesus had great spiritual insight, even though we wouldn't accept that he was God or that he was raised from the dead. We would probably believe that what he taught lives on after his death, and because of his example there is hope for the world. Almost all Christians would say that Jesus was a good man in the fullest sense. Even Muslims, who do not believe that Jesus is the Son of God, would agree.

If we were to hold the view that Jesus was the Son of God, we would make Jesus' teaching central to the way we lived our lives. We would know that we would be forgiven for things we get wrong and we could call on him for help in times of trouble. We would become involved in telling other people about Jesus, and we wouldn't fear death because we would believe Jesus conquered it.

Activity

Hold a secret ballot to see who people in your class think Jesus was. Draw a graph to show your class's views.

Discuss

In groups, discuss the three views. Is one argument more convincing than the others? Can they all be right?

Summary of Topic 1: God's relationship with the world

Discuss

1 Which story do you think explains the character of God most clearly?

2 Are there stories where God's character seems very different?

Drawing it all together …

In many ways, God should be unknowable and yet, according to the Bible, he chose to make himself known to the world. He did not do it in one magnificent revelation because no one would be able to take it in. Instead he spoke to individual people in different situations and acted through them. In this way it became possible to put together a picture of what he is like. Right from the start it was clear that God wanted a relationship with people. He wasn't just a remote being whom they worshipped from afar and never got to know. He made demands of them and laid down principles for living, the most important being that they should worship him alone and not be side-tracked into other religious practices.

In the Old Testament this meant the pagan cults like Baal worship, but in the New Testament it meant something a little more abstract. It meant having faith that Jesus was God's son and that he had the power to save people just as they had been saved in the past. The overall message is that God is in control of his world and that his plan for the people he made meant intervening in their lives. God's saving action would bring them to a place where they could turn back to him.

Activity

Here are some descriptions of God's nature:

Creator Powerful Faithful

Just/Righteous All knowing Holy

Merciful Compassionate Saviour

1 Make a chart of the stories in Topic 1 and link these descriptions to the stories. (You may find one word applies to more than one story.)

2 Think of three more ways to describe what God is like and add them to the chart.

Discuss

In how many different ways did God save people in these stories?

Activity

Think about the stories in Topic 1 as a whole. List the ways in which you think God has acted and make a pyramid to show the ones in which you think he acted most powerfully.

Topic 2 — Human responses to God

In Topic 2 we will study the way human beings behave towards each other, towards the created world and towards God. The stories reveal what people are like and how they react in certain situations. They reflect personal encounters with God and with Jesus and discuss what happens when people come into conflict with what God demands or expects of them. It also examines what it is that makes people respond to God in a positive way that leads to repentance and a change of direction in their lives. This topic explores what it means to have faith and to commit oneself to the challenges of a life lived in obedience to God. It investigates how people can do God's work in the world both environmentally and socially.

What are human beings like?

How should we react to God's commands?

Is human nature basically flawed?

What makes us happy?

What things that other people do, make us angry?

If you could have one wish for the world what would it be?

What does it mean to be committed to something?

What should happen if we disobey authority?

What difference does it make whether we live a moral life or not? Is there an advantage to being good?

To what extent do we have a responsibility to the world and to people?

What kind of person do you want to become?

Activity

In groups, discuss these questions.

Make a collage that addresses the questions you think are most important. You can use pictures and text from articles in magazines and online to illustrate your ideas. Add to the display as you work through Topic 2.

2.1 The first responses: Adam and Eve; Cain and Abel

This chapter looks at Adam and Eve and their two sons Cain and Abel. The story of Adam and Eve begins in the Garden of Eden where they enjoy a perfect relationship with God, with each other and with the natural world. It continues with an account of how that all changed when they set themselves up in opposition to God. They had to leave the Garden and all it offered to make a living for themselves in the harsh outside environment. Their sons Cain and Abel worked the land, tending the sheep and growing crops, but their relationship with each other was broken by bitterness and envy on the part of Cain. It ended with the murder of Abel and the expulsion of Cain from the farm where they lived.

These three stories show what humans are like and how they respond to God's commands. They also illustrate what happens when they disobey him and move away from God's purpose for them and for the world.

Starter
What do humans need to be happy?

2.1a The Garden of Eden: Genesis 2.4–25

Read **Genesis 2.4–25**.

Using just the verses in each box for your answers, follow the instructions.

A   God made the earth. Genesis 2.4–6

Make a list of what he created.

What was missing?

B   God made Adam and the Garden. Genesis 2.7–14

Describe the Garden God made.

How did God make Adam?

▲ Adam and Eve in the Garden of Eden from the Vatican museum.

stewards/stewardship – looking after the world for God and for future generations.

C   God made Adam a steward of the Garden. Genesis 2.15–18

Make a list of the instructions God gave Adam about the Garden.

What did God see was missing in Adam's life?

D   God made the living creatures. Genesis 2.19–20

Describe how God involved Adam in his creation.

Why were the living creatures not enough to make him happy?

E   God made Eve. Genesis 2.21–5

Describe how God made Eve.

In what ways could Adam and Eve be suitable companions for each other?

Understanding the story of the Garden of Eden

God's creative action

God reveals his power to bring to life what was lifeless. He uses the fabric of the earth to create a man. The words 'dust to dust', used at funerals, are a reference to humans being part of the earth from the beginning, and returning to it at the end. God's breath is the life-giving force that gives them independent existence.

The Garden of Eden means the garden of delight, with God and humans living and working harmoniously together. The presence of the tree of knowledge of good and evil shows that God has put moral restriction in place. This was the condition of Adam's existence – if he eats from the tree, he will die. Human beings can't decide for themselves what is right and what is wrong. The structure of good and evil is an unchangeable part of the world.

At first, everything was wonderful. Adam had a land overflowing with bounty. God put Adam into the world to take care of it and he gave responsibility for animal welfare to him. Humans were not meant to live alone and so, in a beautifully symbolic way, Eve arrives on the scene as Adam's partner. In a world where equality of women with men was rare, this is a significant detail. Here at last was another human being to stand at Adam's side and share in the delights and responsibilities of the Garden. The story teaches that human beings need companionship of their own kind. Men and women were made for each other, to live together and raise a family. A Christian marriage service uses part of this story: 'For this reason a man will leave his father and mother and be united with his wife, and they will become one flesh.'

What do you know? **AO1**

1 Describe the Garden of Eden.
2 Describe the role God intended for humans in the world.
3 What evidence is there that God wanted human beings to be happy?
4 What command did God give about the tree of knowledge of good and evil?

What do you understand? **AO2**

5 Explain what the story teaches about human beings.
6 Explain what the story teaches about how humans should treat animals.

What do you think? **AO3**

7 Are men and women equal in today's world?
8 What is the role of animals in the lives of humans?

Theology in action – stewards of the Earth

A Rocha is a Christian organisation that promotes **nature conservation**. It was founded by Peter and Miranda Harris in 1983 because they believed that one of their tasks, as Christians, was to follow God's command to the first humans and take care of the world as his stewards. They believe that God cares deeply about what happens to the Earth. As it says in Psalm 50, 'Every animal of the forest is mine, and the cattle on the thousand hills. I know every bird in the mountains'. They hold that the environment is also an issue of justice as it is usually the poor who suffer first when the climate changes. By actively working for the good of all living things, they aim to persuade humans that they can make the world into a better place. They believe that their work is part of God's great plan to redeem the whole of creation.

Activity

Find examples from magazines, newspapers and the internet and create a poster to show how human beings have been good stewards.

2.1b The Fall: Genesis 3

Starter
Are humans basically good or basically bad?

Read **Genesis 3**.

The story falls into three sections:

The snake tempts
Eve to disobey God.

Both Adam and Eve
eat the fruit.

God confronts the snake,
Adam and Eve

What do you know? (AO1)

1 What persuasive arguments did the serpent use to tempt Eve?
2 Describe what happened after Adam and Eve had eaten the forbidden fruit.
3 What were the consequences of their disobedience?

What do you understand? (AO2)

4 What do we learn about human nature from Adam and Eve's behaviour in the story?
5 Why was the serpent successful in his temptation of Eve?

What do you think? (AO3)

6 Why did Eve listen to the serpent?

Activity
Rewrite the story in any way you like. For example, as a diary entry, a play, or as a straight narrative.

Understanding the story of the Fall

This is a story about greed and selfish ambition on the part of Adam and Eve; and justice, compassion and mercy on the part of God.

The camouflaged, sinuous serpent makes a perfect symbol for the devil. It invites Eve to doubt God's word and subtly turns God's command into a temptation. It tempts her to do something wrong and call it justifiable and right – to redraw the moral compass. The fruit is tempting because it seems to grant power, but it is a false power: just saying something is good or right does not make it so. Only God has this power.

The eating of the fruit is a picture of human failure and speaks across the centuries to people today. Women are often seen as temptresses and men portrayed as weak: that is the picture here. Both of them could have resisted but each made their own decision and brought upon themselves the consequences of what the Bible calls '**sin**'. Neither one is more guilty than the other.

As soon as they take the first bite, they realise something has changed. Walking with God in the garden, as his favoured companions, is no longer to be enjoyed. The knowledge that they have done wrong, no matter how hard they tried to justify it, makes them feel guilt and shame. Nakedness in this context has nothing to do with sexuality; it is a powerful symbol for shame. Without clothes we are defenceless and vulnerable, and the world can see us as we are. This is how Adam and Eve felt and that is why they tried to hide from God. In doing so, they discovered that there is no hiding from him.

> **Discuss**
> The consequences of their disobedience led to suffering for Adam and Eve as they had to struggle to survive outside the garden. Do we cause our own suffering?

The 'punishments' that God hands out to Adam, Eve and the serpent highlight the change in the way the world will now have to work. Human beings can no longer be trusted to do the right thing. The serpent, who tried to take the place of God in his conversation with Eve, had to be brought down.

- The serpent's punishment was humiliation – to be trampled on. From now on, people would try to do right but be tempted to do wrong. It also represented the way God's creation would now be at odds with itself.

- The woman's punishment was to know (experience) suffering. Childbirth is the most fundamental human process but it is painful. There would also be a shift in her relationship with the man. The easy equality would disappear and he would exert his authority over her.

- The man's punishment was to sweat and toil to survive. In imposing his mastery over it, he would change the balance between human beings and the natural world.

The beginning of God's plan of salvation

The giving of clothes is a symbol of God's mercy. He gives people a 'covering' for their shame, a way of still being able to approach God. But it is not a thing people can do for themselves; it is God's gift which makes it possible.

The expulsion from the Garden is a symbol of how things have changed. The world where everything was good has been spoiled and can never be recaptured. It will only be by God's grace that humans can come back into a relationship with him. The main theme of the Bible is how God reverses the consequences of what happened and saves human beings from the snare of sin.

What do you know? **AO1**

1 What is 'sin'?
2 Compare the life Adam and Eve had in the Garden with what they might expect outside it.

What do you understand? **AO2**

3 Explain the significance of the tree of knowledge.
4 What does the story teach about how human beings react to God?
5 Why did God punish Adam and Eve?
6 Explain why we read the story of the Fall at Christmas.
7 Explain how Adam and Eve's relationship with God changed after they had eaten the fruit.

What do you think? **AO3**

8 Do human beings bring all their suffering on to themselves?
9 Does punishment help people to change their ways? (See Section 2, page 133.)

Theology in action – living in a 'fallen' world

All religions attempt to answer the problem of evil and suffering in the world. Nearly all attribute it to wrongdoing or 'sin'. Whether you take the story of the Fall literally or symbolically, its message is about the breaking apart of everything that was held together in Eden – God's relationship with his creation, and his creation's relationship with itself. Humans are part of that broken system and they can't fix it. God fixes it. In the Bible, the theme of **salvation**, God's saving action to bring his creation back into harmony with himself, starts here. It reaches its pinnacle with the **crucifixion** and **Resurrection** of Jesus.

> How does the Christian belief about the origin of evil and suffering help people to understand and deal with suffering in their own lives?

> Some people think suffering is a punishment for wrongdoing, as seen in the Old Testament. However, in the New Testament, when Jesus is asked this same question in the context of a man born blind, he says that is not the man's sin nor his parents' sin. It shows God's power to overcome the bad things in life.

During the Second World War, millions of Jews were taken to concentration camps and held in terrible conditions. John Humphrys asked Jonathan Sacks, who was the Chief Rabbi at the time, where God was in these camps. He answered that God was there in anyone who offered comfort and hope, who brought light into the darkness.

Another reason given for the presence of evil and suffering in the world is that God gave us free will. Adam and Eve were free to make their own decisions. We always have a choice and we, and others, have to live by the consequences of those choices. One example is the way we abuse the environment. This has led to increasing climate change which means places like Bangladesh suffer serious floods. A trivial example might be when someone in your class misbehaves and everyone suffers by being kept in at break.

A third reason given to explain why bad things happen is that it makes us appreciate the good things and encourages us to grow as human beings. A person who has lived through hardship has a depth of character that is not there in someone who hasn't. St Paul, a pioneering Christian missionary, wrote in one of his letters that suffering produces endurance, endurance produces character, and character produces hope – hope for the future.

▲ The concentration camp of Birkenau near Cracow in Poland.

Activity

Comment on these suggestions – that suffering is as a result of sin, that it comes because people have free will and can choose to do things that cause it, and that it makes people appreciate the good times and develop character. Is one argument more compelling than the others? Is there an element of truth in all three or does none of them convince you? Give reasons to support your answer.

2.1c Cain and Abel: Genesis 4.1–16

Starter
What kinds of things make you jealous?

The story of Cain's jealousy of his brother Abel ended in murder. You can read the whole story in **Genesis 4.1–16**.

ADAM AND EVE SLEPT TOGETHER. EVE BECAME PREGNANT AND GAVE BIRTH TO A SON, CALLED CAIN.

LATER SHE HAD ANOTHER SON, ABEL.

CAIN GREW UP TO WORK THE SOIL; ABEL BECAME A SHEPHERD.

IN TIME, CAIN BROUGHT SOME OF HIS HARVEST AS AN OFFERING TO GOD. ABEL BROUGHT THE BEST LAMB OF HIS FLOCK.

GOD WAS PLEASED WITH ABEL'S OFFERING, BUT NOT WITH CAIN'S. ABEL WAS A GOOD MAN, A MAN OF FAITH, BUT GOD COULD SEE THE DARKNESS IN CAIN'S HEART.

CAIN WAS FURIOUS.

AND SO GOD SAID:

WHY SO ANGRY, CAIN? NO NEED TO SCOWL IF YOU HAVE DONE RIGHT.

IF NOT, SIN IS CROUCHING BY THE DOOR OF YOUR LIFE. IT WANTS TO CONTROL YOU.

BUT YOU MUST FIGHT IT!

BUT CAIN REFUSED TO LISTEN TO GOD. HE BURNED WITH RAGE.

ALLOWING HIS ANGER TO RULE HIM, HE PLOTTED AGAINST HIS BROTHER...

Read **Genesis 4.8–16** to find out what happens next.

Activity

Make a flow chart outlining the events that led up to Cain becoming a nomad.

Discuss

Is remorse the worst feeling there is?

What do you know?

1 Describe the events that led to the murder of Abel.

2 How did Cain answer God's question about the whereabouts of Abel?

3 How did God know what Cain had done?

4 What were the consequences of Cain's action?

5 Outline the conversation between God and Cain after he had murdered Abel.

What do you understand?

AO2

6 How did God try to bring Cain back into a good relationship with him before the murder of Abel?

7 Suggest at least two reasons why God put a mark of protection on Cain.

8 What does the story teach about human nature?

Understanding the story of Cain and Abel

sacrifice – giving up something of value as a gesture of thanksgiving or repentance

In the story of Adam and Eve, the sin is that of disobedience, pride and self-will; in this story, it is jealousy. Once sin has been committed it has a knock-on effect and affects the development of human character. Adam and Eve were farming with their two sons, Cain and Abel, both of whom had important jobs. These reflected the two different types of farming in those days – animal rearing and agriculture. A sacrificial system had developed, showing they still kept up a relationship with God. By offering something in sacrifice they showed their gratitude for his provision, and asked for his protection against bad things happening. Only the best was good enough and Abel gave the fat from the firstborn of his flock. Offering the firstborn was an act of faith because the other lambs had yet to be born safely. Cain offered some of his grain.

Why did God reject Cain's sacrifice?

Rejecting Cain's sacrifice seems on the surface to be rather unfair. Anyone who studies the Bible will quickly see, however, that God looks at the heart – at motives and character – before looking at the action. The story shows Cain to be an angry young man with a violent temper. God pointed out that this attitude was at the root of his problems and warned him that sin was waiting like a wild animal to overtake him. That's the trouble with a sin like envy or anger: a person can be overcome by it and then it leads to other and greater sin, as it did in this case. If Cain's behaviour and attitude changed, God would accept his sacrifice.

Why did Cain kill Abel?

Cain was envious of Abel's good relationship with God. He must have been aware of his bad temper but he blamed his brother for causing his anger and jealousy. His anger may also reflect the natural antagonism between agricultural and sheep farming. Whatever was at the root of the rift between the brothers, it led to murder.

GOD WAS PLEASED WITH ABEL'S OFFERING, BUT NOT WITH CAIN'S. ABEL WAS A GOOD MAN, A MAN OF FAITH, BUT GOD COULD SEE THE DARKNESS IN CAIN'S HEART.

CAIN WAS FURIOUS.

God's response

Cain's reaction to God's question is a typical reaction of a guilty person. He was defensive, aggressive and wanted to forget what he had done. God said he had heard Abel's blood crying from the ground. This symbolic language means that God knew and cared that an innocent person had suffered at the hands of someone violent. Blood is a symbol of life. It was only when Cain knew that he had been found out that he owned up to what he had done. It is interesting that God did not strike Cain dead for what he had done. Under Old Testament law, the punishment for murder is death. Instead, God rehabilitated him. He sent him away from his home and family and the protection they offered, into the no-man's land around. Any foreign tribes would kill Cain if they found him on their land and Cain was terrified. So God had mercy on him and put a protective mark on him. The mark may have been a contagious skin disease, which would explain why someone coming into contact with him would die. Whatever it was, it reassured Cain and gave him the chance to try again.

What do you understand? **AO2**

1 Explain why God accepted Abel's sacrifice but not Cain's.

2 What does God mean when he says that Abel's blood is crying out to him from the ground?

3 What should Cain's response have been to God's rejection of his offering?

4 What does the story teach about God?

5 What do we learn about human behaviour from this story?

> **Essay practice**
>
> 'A life for a life is fair. God should not have given Cain a second chance.' Do you agree? Give reasons for your answer. Show that you have considered more than one point of view.

What do you think? **AO3**

6 Anger is described as being like a wild animal crouching at the door, waiting to pounce and devour. How is this a good description of what happens when we get angry?

2.2 Abraham's response

Starter
What things do we value the most and under what circumstances would we be prepared to give them up?

God had a special relationship with Abraham. He spoke to him when he was living in Haran, before he had any children, and told him to move all his belongings and his family to a land that God would show him. Abraham responded by obeying God. God promised that Abraham would have many descendants, but Isaac was his only legitimate son and he had been born to Abraham in his old age. Isaac was his only hope. This is why the story of God demanding this special boy was such a huge test of Abraham's faith in God's promise. Abraham's response was again one of obedience and faith.

The near sacrifice of Isaac: Genesis 22.1–19

1 Some time later God tested Abraham. He said to him, 'Abraham!'

'Here I am!' he replied.

2 Then God said, 'Take your son, your only son, whom you love – Isaac – and go to the region of Moriah. Sacrifice him there as a burnt offering on a mountain I will show you.'

3 Early the next morning Abraham got up and loaded his donkey. He took with him two of his servants and his son Isaac. When he had cut enough wood for the burnt offering, he set out for the place God had told him about. 4 On the third day Abraham looked up and saw the place in the distance. 5 He said to his servants, 'Stay here with the donkey while I and the boy go over there. We will worship and then we will come back to you.'

6 Abraham took the wood for the burnt offering and placed it on his son Isaac, and he himself carried the fire and the knife. As the two of them went on together, 7 Isaac spoke up and said to his father Abraham, 'Father?'

'Yes, my son?' Abraham replied.

'The fire and wood are here,' Isaac said, 'but where is the lamb for the burnt offering?'

8 Abraham answered, 'God himself will provide the lamb for the burnt offering, my son.' And the two of them went on together.

9 When they reached the place God had told him about, Abraham built an altar there and arranged the wood on it. He bound his son Isaac and laid him on the altar, on top of the wood. 10 Then he reached out his hand and took the knife to slay his son.

11 But the angel of the Lord called out to him from heaven, 'Abraham! Abraham!'

'Here I am,' he replied.

12 'Do not lay a hand on the boy,' he said. 'Do not do anything to him. Now I know that you fear God, because you have not withheld from me your son, your only son.'

13 Abraham looked up and there in a thicket he saw a ram caught by its horns. He went over and took the ram and sacrificed it as a burnt offering instead of his son. 14 So Abraham called that place The Lord Will Provide. And to this day it is said, 'On the mountain of the Lord it will be provided.'

15 The angel of the Lord called to Abraham from heaven a second time, 16 and said, 'I swear by myself, declares the Lord, that because you have done this and have not withheld your son, your only son, 17 I will surely bless you and make your descendants as numerous as the stars in the sky and as the sand on the seashore. Your descendants will take possession of the cities of their enemies, 18 and through your offspring all nations on earth will be blessed, because you have obeyed me.'

19 Then Abraham returned to his servants, and they set off together for Beersheba. And Abraham stayed in Beersheba.

Genesis 22.1–19

What do you know? AO1

1 Describe Abraham's preparations for his journey with Isaac to Mount Moriah.
2 What questions did Isaac ask his father on the way?
3 Describe what happened when they reached the top of the mountain.
4 What was the promise that God gave Abraham?
5 How did God reward Abraham's faith in him?

What do you understand? AO2

6 In what ways were the events in this story a test?
7 Why does the last picture show a star-studded sky?

Understanding the story of Abraham and Isaac

Background

Offering sacrifices to God formed a central part of Old Testament life, and although the sacrificial system developed mostly after Abraham died, it is a very important part of how the Jewish nation understood their relationship with God. They gave the first fruits of the harvest both as thanksgiving and as an act of faith that God would prosper the whole growing season. The killing of the best of the cattle thanked God for providing pasture and food. Blood was sacred because it represented life, which was the greatest thing anyone could offer. Mountaintops were thought to be nearer God, therefore appropriate places for sacrifices.

The Israelites believed that God took an interest in them that went beyond merely arranging good living conditions. They believed that God cared how they behaved. They soon realised they needed a way to say sorry for the things they did wrong. Over the years new rituals emerged – special sacrifices were offered as a way of making things right with God again. This was called **atonement**. This is the way most Christians understand what happened when Jesus died. It is important to know about this way of thinking because it helps to understand why Jesus' death is seen as a sacrifice for sin. (See page 44.)

The story of the near sacrifice of Isaac continues the biblical theme of God's provision for human beings. He provided the ram to take the place of Isaac. That is why Abraham called the mountain 'The Lord provides'. It was never God's intention that Isaac should die. The emphasis was not on what Abraham gave to God but what God provided for him.

Abraham's faith and God's provision

covenant – an agreement between two parties

God had made a covenant with Abraham that he would be the father of a great nation (Genesis 17). This was before Abraham had any children. In fact, he and his wife Sarah had been trying for decades to have a baby without success. Yet Abraham held fast to his belief in God's promise. Eventually in their old age and against all the odds, they had a son called Isaac. In return, God wanted two specific things from Abraham: his complete trust and his obedience.

Abraham was prepared to give God both those things so when he heard God telling him to give up Isaac, he trusted that God would somehow still fulfil his promise. It was here that God revealed that what he valued most was the state of Abraham's heart. Abraham's motives were pure, his **faith** was solid and his obedience was absolute. It was time for him to experience for himself the faithfulness of the God he had chosen to worship. So, although on the surface this story seems to portray God as a cruel and manipulative being, it is actually the beginning of a special relationship between God and his people and a foretaste of his saving action in the world. He provided a ram for Abraham to sacrifice in place of Isaac, and centuries later, according to Christian belief, God would provide his son Jesus as a sacrifice for all human beings.

The promise goes further. Abraham's descendants would become a nation and through that nation (Israel) the whole world would be blessed. This blessing would come through Jesus who would bring people back into a good relationship with God.

How can we make sense of this story today?

This is a difficult story for people today because it involves what would be considered the grossest possible form of child abuse. Perhaps the questions we need to ask are whether we should always obey God and, if so, how can we know if it really is God speaking? Is Abraham an especially good role model as he lived in a different culture at a different time and, if so, why? On the one hand, if God tells you to do something, it can't be wrong to do it. On the other hand, as with Abraham, it might be a test of faith and resolve, which can only be determined by pursuing what you believe to be God's will until such point as your willing obedience and faith has been established. In the end, Abraham did not kill Isaac and we cannot know for sure what would have happened had God not intervened. Through it all, Abraham was true to himself and true to his God, his faith never wavering, and these are good qualities to aspire to.

The relevance of the story lies in the fact that it shows that God had a plan right from the beginning to bring about salvation, not just in Israel but across all nations.

What do you understand?

AO2

1 Explain the purpose of offering sacrifices.
2 Explain how this story was a test of Abraham's faith.
3 Draw a diagram to show what the story teaches about God.
4 Explain how Abraham's faith would affect people in the future.
5 Explain why God might be more interested in the state of a person's heart than in the ritual of sacrifice.
6 What does the story teach about Abraham's response to God?

faith – confidence and trust in someone or in God

Discuss
Is faith a question of hearing God's true voice or is it a question of taking faith to its extreme, as religious terrorists might do?

Essay practice
'Abraham was wrong even to think about sacrificing his son.' Do you agree? Give reasons for your answer. Show that you have considered more than one point of view.

2.3 David, Bathsheba, Uriah and Nathan

Starter

1 What groups of people have power in your school?

2 Have there ever been occasions when you think they have abused that power?

This chapter is about David and how his immoral behaviour affected the lives of those involved. He was called by God to be king long before he actually became king and up to this point he had been a just ruler. By having an affair with Bathsheba, the wife of one of his serving soldiers, he abused his power. Bathsheba's husband Uriah, by contrast, is shown to be a man of great integrity who stuck by the moral code of his military position. His refusal to compromise led to his death. It was down to Nathan the prophet to expose David's sin.

David and Bathsheba: 2 Samuel 11.1–17

Read the story of David and Bathsheba in **2 Samuel 11.1–17.**

1 In the spring the kings would go out to war. So in the spring David sent out Joab, his servants and all the Israelites. They destroyed the Ammonites and attacked the city of Rabbah. But David stayed in Jerusalem. 2 One evening David got up from his bed. He walked around on the roof of his palace. While he was on the roof, he saw a woman bathing. She was very beautiful. 3 So David sent his servants to find out who she was. A servant answered, 'That woman is Bathsheba daughter of Eliam. She is the wife of Uriah the Hittite.' 4 David sent messengers to bring Bathsheba to him. When she came to him, he had physical relations with her. (Now Bathsheba had purified herself from her monthly period.) Then she went back to her house. 5 But Bathsheba became pregnant. She sent word to David, saying, 'I am pregnant.'

6 So David sent this message to Joab: 'Send Uriah the Hittite to me.' So Joab sent Uriah to David. 7 Uriah came to David. And David asked him how Joab was, how the soldiers were and how the war was going. 8 Then David said to Uriah, 'Go home and rest.'

So Uriah left the palace. The king also sent a gift to him. 9 But Uriah did not go home. He slept outside the door of the palace. He slept there as all the king's officers did.

10 The officers told David, 'Uriah did not go home.'

Then David said to Uriah, 'You came from a long trip. Why didn't you go home?'

11 Uriah said to him, 'The Ark of the Covenant and the soldiers of Israel and Judah are staying in tents. My master Joab and his officers are camping out in the fields. It isn't right for me to go home to eat and drink and have intimate relations with my wife!'

12 David said to Uriah, 'Stay here today. Tomorrow I'll send you back to the battle.' So Uriah stayed in Jerusalem that day and the next. 13 Then David called Uriah to come to see him. Uriah ate and drank with David. David made Uriah drunk, but he still did not go home. That evening Uriah went to sleep with the king's officers outside the king's door.

14 The next morning David wrote a letter to Joab and sent it by Uriah. 15 In the letter David wrote, 'Put Uriah on the front lines where the fighting is worst. Then leave him there alone. Let him be killed in battle.'

16 Joab watched the city and saw where its strongest defenders were. He put Uriah there. 17 The men of the city came out to fight against Joab. Some of David's men were killed. And Uriah the Hittite was one of them.

2 Samuel 11.1–17

What do you know?

1 Describe what happened after David first saw Bathsheba.
2 How did David try to cover up his adultery when he heard Bathsheba was pregnant?
3 Describe how David arranged for Uriah to be killed.
4 What reason did Uriah give for not going home?

What do you understand? AO2

5 What kind of a man was Uriah? Support your answer with evidence from the text.
6 In the final frame of the story strip David says, 'It was as if I'd murdered him myself.' What did he mean?

What do you think? AO3

7 Was Uriah right to disobey his king?

Understanding the story of David and Bathsheba

The role of king in those days was to protect his people from their enemies. The story of David and Bathsheba shows what happens when a leader forgets his role and puts himself first. David thought that being king meant he could do things ordinary people were not allowed to do, in this case taking another man's wife. Today, having an affair with the spouse of a soldier on active service is a court martial offence.

David's sin
Adultery

The fact that Bathsheba lived in a stone house close to the palace implies that she was wealthy and therefore most likely to be married. David was on the roof of his palace, taking a break from his military duties. From there he had a good view of the surrounding roofs and saw a beautiful woman bathing. David made enquiries about her and found out her name and that she was indeed married. She was also well-born – her grandfather was one of David's trusted advisors. So David was not acting in ignorance. Adultery breaks the seventh commandment. The fact that he **coveted** another man's wife also broke the tenth commandment.

covet – to desire something that isn't yours

Attempted deception

Once Bathsheba sent word that she was pregnant, David had to act quickly. There was no doubt that the baby was his because her husband was at war. He made two attempts to persuade Uriah to go home and be with his wife. Passing the baby off as Uriah's would be the easiest way out of his embarrassment. But he had not counted on Uriah's integrity. While a man is on a military campaign and God is fighting with Israel, there are some things that are forbidden; sex is one of them. Uriah would not behave differently from his fellow soldiers therefore David's attempt to deceive him over the paternity of the child failed. Deceit breaks the ninth commandment.

Murder

David used the only option now available to him. He arranged for Uriah to be killed in battle. Murder breaks the sixth commandment.

Abuse of power

David acted wrongly against people who could not fight back. As a man, he was stronger than Bathsheba. As a military leader, he could command Uriah. As king, he had abused his power over two of his subjects. Abuse of power is not specifically mentioned in the Ten Commandments but it goes against a fundamental principle of human behaviour and is implicit in many of the commandments.

▲ David's palace rooftop would have commanded a view over the house roofs around him. They were mostly flat and used for a wide variety of activities.

What do you know? AO1

1 What was the role of a king at this time?
2 Make a list of all the things David did wrong in this story.

What do you understand? AO2

3 Explain how David's actions were an abuse of his power.
4 Explain what the story teaches about human nature.
5 Explain what the story teaches about David.

What do you think? AO3

6 Have people today lost their sense of right and wrong as David had? Give reasons to support your answer.

David and Nathan: 2 Samuel 12.1–14

1 The Lord sent Nathan to David. When he came to him, he said, 'There were two men in a certain town, one rich and the other poor. 2 The rich man had a very large number of sheep and cattle, 3 but the poor man had nothing except one little ewe lamb that he had bought. He raised it, and it grew up with him and his children. It shared his food, drank from his cup and even slept in his arms. It was like a daughter to him.

4 'Now a traveller came to the rich man, but the rich man refrained from taking one of his own sheep or cattle to prepare a meal for the traveller who had come to him. Instead, he took the ewe lamb that belonged to the poor man and prepared it for the one who had come to him.'

5 David burned with anger against the man and said to Nathan, 'As surely as the Lord lives, the man who did this deserves to die! 6 He must pay for that lamb four times over, because he did such a thing and had no pity.'

7 Then Nathan said to David, 'You are the man! This is what the Lord, the God of Israel, says: "I anointed you king over Israel, and I delivered you from the hand of Saul. 8 I gave your master's house to you, and your master's wives into your arms. I gave you all Israel and Judah. And if all this had been too little, I would have given you even more. 9 Why did you despise the word of the Lord by doing what is evil in his eyes? You struck down Uriah the Hittite with the sword and took his wife to be your own. You killed him with the sword of the Ammonites. 10 Now, therefore, the sword shall never depart from your house, because you despised me and took the wife of Uriah the Hittite to be your own."

11 'This is what the Lord says: "Out of your own household I am going to bring calamity on you. Before your very eyes I will take your wives and give them to one who is close to you, and he will sleep with your wives in broad daylight. 12 You did it in secret, but I will do this thing in broad daylight before all Israel."'

13 Then David said to Nathan, 'I have sinned against the Lord.'

Nathan replied, 'The Lord has taken away your sin. You are not going to die. 14 But because by doing this you have shown utter contempt for the Lord, the son born to you will die.'

2 Samuel 12.1–14

What do you know? — AO1

1 Outline the parable Nathan told David.
2 What was David's response to the parable?
3 Describe how Nathan exposed David as the man in the parable.
4 What were to be the consequences of David's sin?

Activity
Write a parable that Nathan might have told if this situation had taken place today.

What do you understand? — AO2

5 Explain the parallel between the man in Nathan's parable and David.
6 What sin was particularly exposed in Nathan's parable?

What do you think? — AO3

7 How was Nathan's choice of using a parable a good way of getting God's point across?

Understanding Nathan's parable: 2 Samuel 12.1–14

Nathan was a prophet. Prophets were not always popular as their messages from God were seldom to people's liking. However, they were greatly respected and acted as advisers to leaders and kings. This enabled Nathan to tell David about God's anger.

David had allowed his physical desire to rule his head. When he heard Nathan's parable, he properly condemned the man in the story for his actions. He even spoke of the death penalty although the usual punishment was a fine of four times the lamb's value.

David must have been shocked when Nathan said at the end, 'You are that man' but David realised then that what he had done was unacceptable. David showed great remorse as he saw that he had not just hurt the people under his protection, but he had sinned against God. Nathan pointed out to David that God had given him everything he could want: deliverance from Saul, Saul's kingdom and all his wives. Yet David wanted more and used his position as king to get it.

Nathan told David what the consequences would be. It is an old idea that punishment for evil deeds goes on to the next generation. It is important to distinguish between punishment and consequences. Jesus taught that a person's suffering was not the result of something their parents had done wrong. However, all actions, good and bad, have consequences and these can last for several generations. Children are greatly influenced by the way their parents behave and by the views they hold. David's family was a violent one. His own son Absolom took up arms against him and was killed, to David's terrible grief (2 Samuel 18.14–15).

What do you know? AO1

1 What was Nathan's role?
2 What did David realise about his actions?

What do you understand? AO2

3 In what way was Nathan courageous?
4 Explain the point Nathan was making to David in his conversation with him.
5 Explain what this story teaches about how people react to God.

Essay practice

'Power goes hand in hand with responsibility.' Do you agree? Give reasons for your answer. Show that you have considered more than one point of view.

What do you think? AO3

6 Nathan prophesies that some of David's descendants will die violent deaths. Is there a difference between punishment for and the consequences of a wrong action? Give reasons to support your answer.

2.4 Responses to Jesus' parables

This chapter is about the way Jesus used parables in his teaching and how those who listened to them responded. A parable is a story that gets a point across, and Jesus told many of them. If he had stuck to teaching abstract theological truths, he would quickly have lost the crowd's interest. Instead he concentrated on real life experiences. Stories from everyday life stick in people's minds. No two people come to exactly the same conclusions about the meaning of the parables. This leads to richness in the Church's teaching. Jesus gave people the freedom to work things out for themselves and discover what God was saying to them in their own lives.

In the parable of **the good Samaritan**, Jesus answers the question 'who is my neighbour?' and makes the important point that one's neighbour is anyone in need, regardless of who they are or where they come from. The parable of **the lost son** is about human nature and the love and forgiveness of God. It is also about an obsession with the letter of the law, which can lead a person to forget God's grace, mercy and love.

2.4a The parable of the good Samaritan: Luke 10.25–37

> **Starter**
> What makes a good neighbour?

25 On one occasion an expert in the law stood up to test Jesus. 'Teacher,' he asked, 'what must I do to inherit eternal life?'

26 'What is written in the Law?' he replied. 'How do you read it?'

27 He answered, 'Love the Lord your God with all your heart and with all your soul and with all your strength and with all your mind'; and, 'Love your neighbour as yourself.'

28 'You have answered correctly,' Jesus replied. 'Do this and you will live.'

29 But he wanted to justify himself, so he asked Jesus, 'And who is my neighbour?'

30 In reply Jesus said: 'A man was going down from Jerusalem to Jericho, when he was attacked by robbers. They stripped him of his clothes, beat him and went away, leaving him half dead. 31 A priest happened to be going down the same road, and when he saw the man, he passed by on the other side. 32 So too, a Levite, when he came to the place and saw him, passed by on the other side. 33 But a Samaritan, as he travelled, came where the man was; and when he saw him, he took pity on him. 34 He went to him and bandaged his wounds, pouring on oil and wine. Then he put the man on his own donkey, brought him to an inn and took care of him. 35 The next day he took out two denarii and gave them to the innkeeper.

'Look after him,' he said, 'and when I return, I will reimburse you for any extra expense you may have.'

36 'Which of these three do you think was a neighbour to the man who fell into the hands of robbers?'

37 The expert in the law replied, 'The one who had mercy on him.'

Jesus told him, 'Go and do likewise.'

Luke 10.25–37

Activity

Write a play that puts the story of the good Samaritan into the contemporary world. Think who you might cast as your Samaritan and your religious leaders.

What do you know? AO1

1 What happened to the man who was travelling to Jericho?

2 Describe the behaviour of the priest and the Levite.

3 What did the Samaritan do?

4 Describe the conversation Jesus had with the teacher of the Law at the end of the parable.

5 What question had the teacher of the Law asked Jesus that prompted his telling of this parable?

What do you understand? AO2

6 Do you think Jesus' reply answered the question asked by the teacher of the law? Give reasons to support your answer.

Understanding the parable of the good Samaritan

This is a great story because, to teach about being loving towards each other, Jesus chooses two groups of people who hate each other. The Samaritans and Jews are old enemies. Conflict between them dates from the eighth century BCE. Israel had divided into two kingdoms: the northern kingdom of Israel and the southern kingdom of Judah. The Assyrians invaded Israel, which included Samaria, and the Samaritans intermarried with those who settled there. A hundred years later Judah was invaded and many of its inhabitants were taken into exile. They eventually returned to re-establish their nation, but the time in exile had led to them fixating on purity of race. Ever since then, the Jews in Judah despised the Samaritans for not being proper Jews. There were plenty of arguments between the two groups over the centuries. The Samaritans even had their own place of worship. Pious Jews were so **prejudiced** they even avoided travelling through Samaria if possible which meant making a long detour. For Jesus to make a Samaritan the hero of the story would have been very unexpected, and would certainly have made everyone sit up and think.

prejudice – an opinion based on feelings rather than fact

The purpose of the parable

Jesus told this parable to answer a practical moral question. It was also to impress on his listeners their duty of loving their neighbours as themselves. Jesus had to explain that neighbourliness went much further than people's limited understanding.

The characters in the parable

- The victim was a Jew. The stretch of road between Jerusalem and Jericho was notoriously unsafe for travellers.

- The man who rescued him was a Samaritan.

- The priest and the Levite were Jewish religious leaders but they did not stop to help even their fellow Jew. They probably thought they had good reason. Touching a dead body or contact with blood would have made them ceremonially unclean and caused delay. They would have had to go through the rituals of purification before being able to enter the Temple and carry out their religious duties. The Levite at least went to have a look but was unable to determine whether the man was dead or alive and may not have wanted to take the risk. However, Jesus left his listeners in no doubt that these were not valid reasons.

The meaning of the parable

The lawyer asked what he must do to inherit eternal life. Inheriting something means you don't have to 'do' anything to get it, so eternal life was a gift not something you earned. However, a strict code of behaviour existed in the Jewish religion for those in line to inherit. Jesus knew that the lawyer would know the answer perfectly well so he turned the question back on him by asking what the law said. Essentially it was divided into two main areas: obligations to God and obligations to people. The traditional summary of the law was 'Love God and love your neighbour as yourself' and this was the answer the lawyer gave to Jesus.

He then asked who his neighbour was and instead of being told as he had expected, that his neighbour was his fellow Jew, he was told that his neighbour was anyone in need of his help. This means there is no room for prejudice of any kind.

The parable for today

Prejudice often arises from a fixed mental idea about a group of people, such as the Samaritans, and it is this kind of stereotyping that is a major cause of making some people feel they have no value (see Section 2, page 143). The trouble is that human beings tend to form groups and feel threatened by those not in their group. People coming from abroad usually have a different culture or speak a different language from those in the country they are visiting. This can lead to misunderstandings and the feeling that those from other races are in some way 'inferior'. Some ethnic groups or followers of one religion are sometimes used as scapegoats when something goes wrong – the blame for problems in society is placed unfairly on them, such as the Jews in Nazi Germany in the 1930s. The rise of terrorism in the twenty-first century, and the way the media reports on it, is a good example of how fear can lead to prejudice against one group. Jesus teaches that we all have a duty to help those in need, whoever they are, not just those we think deserve it or those with whom we agree politically, socially or religiously.

Discuss
How do we 'love' ourselves? How therefore should we 'love' others?

Essay practice
'It is impossible to show kindness to people we think deserve everything they get.' Do you agree? Give reasons for your answer. Show that you have considered more than one point of view.

What do you understand? — AO2

1 Why did Jesus tell parables?

2 Why did neither the priest nor the Levite help the man?

3 Explain why Jesus' listeners would not have expected the Samaritan to have helped the man.

4 Suggest a reason why Jesus chose a Samaritan as his hero.

5 Explain how the parable answers the question 'Who is my neighbour?'

What do you think? — AO3

6 Is the parable relevant in the twenty-first century? Give reasons to support your answer.

2.4b The parable of the lost son: Luke 15.11–32

Read **Luke 15.11–32**.

What do you know?

AO1

1 Describe the two conversations between the father and his younger son at the beginning and at the end of the story.
2 Describe how the younger son used his inheritance.
3 Describe how the younger son came to the point of repentance.
4 Describe the elder son's response to his father's acceptance of his younger brother.

What do you understand?

AO2

5 Why did the younger brother come home?
6 How did the father show his love for both his sons?
7 Why was the elder brother angry?

Understanding the parable of the lost son

This parable was aimed at the **Pharisees**. They had been objecting to the way Jesus associated with tax collectors and other bad characters. The first part of Luke 15 recounts two other parables on the theme of 'lost': the lost coin and the lost sheep. The Pharisees would have been glad to find both a sheep and a silver coin, and their friends would have understood why they were glad.

Jesus said that earthly joy at finding something that had been lost was like the joy felt in heaven when a person came back to God. The father in the story was right to expect his elder son to join in the celebrations when the lost son returned. The elder son thought his father was too soft and that his father's behaviour was grossly unfair on him.

In the time of Jesus, to demand your inheritance was the same as saying you wished your parents were dead. The younger son's request was a terrible insult to his father, who would have had every right to refuse him. The parable is about love, mercy, repentance and forgiveness.

The meaning of the parable: The elder son

The elder son symbolised the **Pharisees** whom Jesus said were out of sympathy with God and in danger of excluding themselves from the heavenly **feast**.

- Just as the elder son was indignant with the father for spending time and money on his bad younger brother, so the Pharisees were indignant that Jesus should spend time with **sinners**. Like the elder son, they were not glad when these sinners repented.

- Like the elder son, the Pharisees were proud of working hard at keeping the commandments, but it never made them feel joyful and they were still unsure whether God accepted them.

- The parable pointed out that in welcoming home the lost son, the elder son would not lose out on anything. 'All that I have is yours' said the father, but the elder son had no sense of being an heir. He talked of having worked 'like a slave' for years. This had never been the father's intention; the elder son was supposed to enjoy working with and being with his father.

The meaning of the parable: The younger son

The younger son represented sinners, those Jesus called 'lost'. He broke all the rules but then, realising the desperate situation he was in, said he was sorry.

- The younger son pleased himself, made sure he was far away from his family and generally behaved in an irresponsible and immoral way. When things are good and you are pursuing a life of pleasure, it is easy to forget about what really matters.

- The famine symbolises hard times. He had used up his father's resources and had nothing. His so-called friends wouldn't help him and he ended up on a pig farm in extreme poverty and distress. It was at this low point that he remembered his father – as many people remember God – and the wealth and freedom of his father's house. At the same time he acknowledged that he did not deserve to be forgiven. This is what is meant by 'repentance'. But he also realised that he *could* go back to his father. That is the hope that people like the tax collectors and other outcasts felt in the presence of Jesus.

- The son went back home and the father not only received him but welcomed him with open arms, forgiving everything he had done and accepting him back into the family as a son. This was the message that Jesus wanted to convey through this part of the parable. No matter how bad a person is, if they truly repent, God will forgive them and bring them back into his kingdom. This is called **redemption** or **salvation**.

The meaning of the parable: The father

The father symbolised God. He had two sons, one troublesome and the other good, but he loved them both equally and they were both his heirs.

- The father accepted his son just as he was – filthy and in rags, symbolic of sin and shame. He even embraced him. He gave him a new set of clothes as befitted a son and an heir and gave him a family ring. This is symbolic of how God accepts people into his kingdom. What they were before, however bad, is not important; it is who they are now that matters. This is called grace. Grace is God's loving mercy when it is undeserved.

- The father showed his love and grace by allowing his younger son his freedom, by watching every day for his return and not giving up on him, and finally by forgiving him and taking him back with great joy. He also showed his love towards his elder son when he pleaded with him to come in to the feast. He did not want him to miss out.

What do you understand? **AO2**

1 Why is the younger son described as 'lost'?

2 Explain how the Pharisees were like the elder brother.

3 Explain what the parable teaches about what God requires of human beings.

4 What does the parable teach about human nature?

5 What does the parable teach about the Kingdom of God?

What do you think? **AO3**

6 Should the father have forgiven his younger son so easily? Give reasons to support your answer.

Essay practice
'We should always forgive others despite what they have done.' Do you agree? Give reasons for your answer. Show that you have considered more than one point of view.

2.5 Responses to Jesus

This last chapter is about how people responded to Jesus. The disciples lived normal working lives until they met him and he asked them to join him. The Roman centurion recognised authority when he saw it in Jesus and it fuelled his faith. Zacchaeus was a total outcast in his community in Jericho but Jesus invited himself into his house and into his life. The rich young man who came to Jesus so full of enthusiasm could not commit when it came to the crunch.

2.5a The call of the disciples: Luke 5.1–11

Starter
How might Peter's skill as a fisherman help him in his new vocation as a 'fisher of men'?

▲ A modern fisherman on the Sea of Galilee.

What do you know? `AO1`

1 Describe the events that led up to Peter letting down his nets.
2 Describe what happened when Jesus got into the boat.
3 Describe Peter's response to Jesus.

What do you understand? `AO2`

4 How does Jesus change Peter's life for ever?
5 How did Jesus' request to Peter demand both action and faith?

Narrator: Jesus attracted people who liked to listen to him telling them stories. However, most of them didn't really understand what it meant to follow Jesus. In this play, Jesus shows how his disciples must be: obedient, willing to give up everything they have, and willing to serve others.

On the shores of the Sea of Galilee …

Jesus: Hi, Pete! Can we push this boat further out? Let's go fishing.

Simon Peter: Actually, me and the lads worked all night and caught nothing … not a sausage. But seeing as how you ask us, we'll give it another whirl. *(shouts)* Hey! Guys! Oy, Johnny, Jamie! Give us a hand. We're going out again.

James: What? You're kidding, right?

Simon Peter: Would I joke about a thing like this?

Man from other boat: I'm with you Pete! Count me in!

Simon Peter: Right … that's far enough. Chuck us the end of that rope, John.

James: On the count of three then, lads! One … two … three …

John: Will you look at this! I've never seen so many fish.

Simon Peter: Wow! Awesome!

John: Er … looks like we've caught a fish or two.

James: We're very low in the water. We need to get back to the shore immediately!

John: *(shouting to other boat)* You look like you're in the same boat. Better hurry!

Man from other boat: In the same boat! Ha ha! Very funny. This lot'll put food into my kids' mouths for a long time. Good tip off, I'd say!

Simon Peter: I don't think I can handle this, Jesus. I'm only a humble guy. I'm … like … not a particularly good sort of bloke. You'd be better off not hanging around people like me.

Jesus: Believe me, Peter, you're exactly the kind of person I want. But forget the fish; from now on you'll be catching men!

Read the full story in **Luke 5.1–11.**

Understanding the call of the disciples

Jesus calls the first disciples

> **Simon Peter**: His response to Jesus was one of humility. He was aware of being sinful but wrongly assumed Jesus wouldn't be interested in him. In another story Jesus gave Simon another name – Peter, which in Greek means 'rock'. He told Peter that he would build his community of believers on Peter's own life of witness, which would be as strong as a rock.

> This story is about how Jesus 'called' the first disciples. The word '**call**' is special. Christians often talk about being 'called' by God to do a specific job, just as Jesus asked his disciples to do a job for him. A call can be referred to as a **vocation**.

Jesus often sat in a boat to teach. It gave him space and enabled everyone to hear what he was saying. Teachers traditionally sat down to teach, unlike today, when they stand up. Luke calls the Sea of Galilee Lake Gennesaret, but they are the same place.

When he had finished teaching, Jesus showed Peter, James and John that his authority affected every area of their lives. So here was Jesus, the carpenter and teacher, telling the fisherman how to do his job, but Peter recognised Jesus' authority because he agreed to let down his nets again, even though they had caught nothing all night. Peter was learning that no area of his life was closed to Jesus. To be a disciple involved allowing Jesus into the heart of his life and recognising that with his power there was nothing he could not achieve. The miracle showed Peter that Jesus must have a very close relationship with God.

It made him deeply aware of his own sinful nature. That was why he fell to his knees and asked Jesus to go away. Fear is a common reaction when people experience the power of God, but Jesus told Peter not to be afraid because he had important work for him: being a fisher of people. The huge number of fish in his net foreshadowed the huge number of people he would bring into God's kingdom.

This was not the first encounter these fishermen had had with Jesus but they now became a team. They were amazed by what had happened and this led them to follow the man who could work such a miracle. When the Bible says they left their nets and followed him, it is unlikely they left the nets full of fish there and then. Rather, they left their way of life and followed Jesus round Israel as he taught people about the Kingdom of God. They realised that their priorities had changed.

Kingdom of God – a spiritual kingdom where God reigns

Essay practice

'Following Jesus means leaving everything and becoming a missionary.' Do you agree? Give reasons for your answer. Show that you have considered more than one point of view.

What do you know? — AO1

1 What is a disciple?

2 How did Peter, James and John show they had become Jesus' disciples?

What do you understand? — AO2

3 Why did Peter change his mind about letting down his nets again?

4 What did Jesus mean by saying he would make Peter a fisher of men?

5 What does the story teach about Peter?

6 What does this story teach about responding to God?

7 Why did Peter fall to his knees in front of Jesus when they caught so much fish?

What do you think? — AO3

8 What does following Jesus mean?

Theology in action – Jackie Pullinger, called to serve God in Hong Kong

Today there are still many people who believe they have been called by God to work in a specific area or lead a specific kind of life. Jackie Pullinger is one of those people. From the time she was at school, she felt God was calling her to tell people about the love of God and his kingdom, just as Peter did two thousand years before her. She believed the place she should go to was Hong Kong.

Jackie was only 22 and no missionary society would take her. However, the vicar of her church said that if she believed God wanted her to work in Hong Kong, she should go.

She put together all her money, and bought a one-way ticket by boat. When she arrived, she got a job teaching music in a primary school. This school was inside a place called the Walled City, which was ruled by gangs of youths called Triads and was the most dangerous place on the island. Everyone was poor in the Walled City and many were on drugs.

Working in the Walled City

Jackie started a youth club and at first the young men and boys who made up the gangs laughed at her and assumed she was rich and would soon go home to the West. When she didn't, and they realised she had no money, they began to take her seriously. People wondered that a woman could do this work. Jackie replied:

'If God had sent a man they'd have beaten him up. Men are threatening to men, but women, especially in Chinese culture, are treated with disregard … They could disregard me because I was not a threat to their maleness and all that made them gangsters.'

Gradually she gained the trust of the young men, and they began to see that she really cared about them. When they wanted to come off drugs, they were able to do so with less pain because Jackie prayed with them.

▲ The Walled City, Hong Kong.

Jackie challenges Goko, the Triad gang's leader

(Poon Sui Jeh is Jackie's Chinese name.)

Goko: Poon Sui Jeh, you have a power that I don't have. If my brothers get hooked on drugs I have them beaten up … but I can't make them quit. But I've watched you. And I believe Jesus can. So I'm going to send all my addicts to you.

Jackie: What you really mean, Goko, is that you want me to help your boys get off drugs so that you can have them back again to work for you. Triads never give up one of their members. Once you become a Triad, you remain one for life. Christians can't serve two bosses; they have to follow either Christ or you. So my answer is no.

Goko: OK. If there is anyone who wants to follow your Jesus, I give up my right to them. You can have all my rotten brothers.

Jackie: That's fine by me; Jesus came for the rotten ones anyhow.

Adapted from Chasing the Dragon by Jackie Pullinger.
Chasing the dragon means smoking opium.

▲ The symbol of the Triads.

Although Jackie never asked for money, people sent it and she was able to open houses like St Stephen's, where drug addicts can go to get off drugs.

Of course, not all addicts became reformed characters overnight, and there were many setbacks. In a recent conference she said that when you are dealing with the poor, you go on giving, even when they steal from you, when they go back on drugs after all your efforts. It is then that you find God's grace.

The Walled City was torn down in 1991 but Jackie's work among the poor and drug addicts goes on. Many of those who have come off drugs stay on in the hostels and work with new arrivals.

Activity

In pairs, discuss the following and write down your thoughts and conclusions:

a) Is it necessary to go abroad to help the poor?

b) Can foreigners like Jackie achieve more than native Christians?

c) What does it mean to have a 'calling'?

d) 'Jesus came for the rotten ones anyhow.' (Jackie Pullinger)

2.5b The centurion: Matthew 8.5–13

Lord, my servant lies at home paralysed, suffering terribly.

Shall I come and heal him?

Lord, I do not deserve to have you come under my roof. But just say the word, and my servant will be healed. For I myself am a man under authority, with soldier under. I tell this one, 'Go,' and he goes; and that one, 'Come,' and he comes. I say to my servant, 'Do this,' and he does it.

Truly I tell you, I have not found anyone in Israel with such great faith. I say to you that many will come from the east and the west, and will take their places at the feast with Abraham, Isaac and Jacob in the kingdom of heaven. But the subjects of the kingdom will be thrown outside, into the darkness, where there will be weeping and gnashing of teeth.

Go! Let it be done just as you believed it would.

And the servant was healed at that moment.

Read this conversation between Jesus and the Roman Centurion, then read the whole of **Matthew 8.5–13**.

What do you know? `AO1`

1 Why did the centurion go to Jesus?
2 Why did he tell Jesus not to come to his house?
3 What examples did the centurion give to show that he understood Jesus' authority?
4 Why was Jesus amazed at his reply?
5 Who did Jesus say would share the heavenly feast with Abraham, Isaac and Jacob?
6 Who might not share the feast after all?

What do you understand? `AO2`

7 Suggest two reasons why Jesus' followers might have been surprised by the event.
8 Why do you think the centurion had such faith in Jesus?

Understanding the story of the centurion

Discuss

Is there a difference between being good and being religious?

There was probably a Roman garrison at Capernaum as it was a large town in Galilee with a reputation for being corrupt. A Roman legion (6000 men) was divided up into centuries (100 men) with a centurion in charge of each. They were the backbone of the Roman army and were responsible for discipline in the ranks. Part of their job was to keep morale high both in peacetime and in war and they were the finest men in the army.

The character of the centurion

The servant would have been a slave in the centurion's household. Slaves had no more value than inanimate objects. It says a lot about this Roman that he cared enough about those who worked for him to seek out Jesus who was a Jew, and ask him to help his slave.

Luke, another gospel writer who recorded this story, says the centurion was highly respected among the Jews, that he had built them a synagogue and respected their beliefs and customs. The centurion knew that for a Jew to enter a Gentile house would make him unclean. He recognised that Jesus had authority rather like his over his soldiers. He told Jesus that he only had to say the word and his servant would be healed; there was no need actually to come to his house. This was in contrast to the Jews' frequent demands for signs and wonders to prove Jesus was the Messiah and sent by God.

Jesus' reaction to the centurion's faith

Jesus was always pleased when someone showed compassion and love and he was impressed by faith. He was astonished when the centurion showed both qualities and it led him to make some surprising remarks to the people around him.

The Jews looked forward to what they called the **Messianic Feast**. It would never have crossed their minds that a Gentile would be invited, especially a Roman, even one the Jews respected. Jesus showed that God is not interested in ancestry but in faith, love and justice, as shown by the centurion. That was the response he wanted. He said that people would come from all over the world, not just Israel, and share in the feast but those originally invited would not attend. This changed everything. Just because the Jews were descended from Abraham, Isaac and Jacob, did not mean their place was secured. They had to live according to the spirit of the law and not use legal loopholes to exploit the poor and the weak. Such people would be thrown out of the feast even if they were 'children of Abraham'. There would be regret when they realised how their greed and arrogance had caused them to miss out on the greatest prize: a place in God's kingdom.

Faith was important – The centurion acted on Jesus' word without insisting that he come home with him. Jesus praised this trust. Faith would allow the centurion entry into the Kingdom of God.

Jesus had God's authority and power – Jesus' word alone had the power to heal. The physical presence of Jesus was not a necessary part of the miracle. This would have huge significance in the future after Jesus' death, resurrection and ascension meant that he was no longer physically present on earth. Christians today have to rely on the word of God and not the physical presence of Jesus.

Lack of faith in God and failure to do what he commanded led to being shut out from his kingdom.

Lessons to learn from the story of Jesus and the centurion

Relying on 'inherited holiness' (being a descendant of Abraham) **was not enough** to gain entry to God's kingdom.

What do you understand? — AO2

1 Explain what the story teaches about the character of the centurion.

2 What does the story teach about faith?

3 Why was the request for Jesus to heal the servant an unusual one?

4 Explain the feast with Abraham, Isaac and Jacob to which Jesus referred?

5 What did Jesus mean by people coming from the east and the west?

6 Explain why the Jews should not take it for granted that they would eat at this banquet.

Essay practice

'You can't be religious without being good.' Do you agree? Give reasons for your answer. Show that you have considered more than one point of view.

What do you think? — AO3

7 What does it mean to be 'religious'?

2.5c Zaccheus: Luke 19.1–10

Read **Luke 19.1–10**.

▲ A 16th century engraving showing Jesus' meeting with Zacchaeus

Discuss

What kind of people would Jesus have associated with today?

What do you know? **AO1**

1 Describe the events that led up to Jesus going to Zacchaeus' house.
2 What was the reaction of the crowd?
3 What did Zacchaeus decide to do?
4 What was Jesus' response?

What do you understand? **AO2**

5 How did Zacchaeus change in this story?

What do you think? **AO3**

6 Is it possible for someone to change their nature?

Activity

1 Think about the painting after you have read the story. Write down three adjectives that might describe the feelings of each of the people in it:
  • Jesus
  • The crowd
  • Zacchaeus
2 In pairs, write a rap about Zacchaeus. Perform it to the class.

Discuss
Should everyone be given a second chance?

Understanding the story of Zacchaeus

Background to the story

Tax collectors in first-century Israel were not paid; they simply collected as much money as they could so that they could have a good sum left over for themselves. They were employed by the Romans. This is the kind of man Zacchaeus would have been – greedy and ruthless – and the citizens of Jericho would have had good reason to despise him. Jericho is south west of Jerusalem, in a particularly hot part of the country situated near the Dead Sea and surrounded by semi desert. However, it was prosperous and an important tax point for traders coming into Israel from the east.

Zacchaeus

Zacchaeus was short, which is why he had to climb a tree if he was to see the great preacher and miracle worker. It would also mean he could observe Jesus discreetly, away from the insults of the crowd, and Jesus himself. Perhaps hope also drove Zacchaeus to see Jesus. Zacchaeus is described as a sinner, an outcast from the Jewish law and therefore avoided by religious people. His lifestyle tells us a lot about human greed but his behaviour teaches us that even the worst person can change. Jesus gave people a second chance and Zacchaeus' own conscience might have prompted him to seek Jesus out. Jesus had already told his disciples how hard it was for a wealthy man to enter the Kingdom of God – but it was not impossible. Zacchaeus accepted Jesus' invitation unlike the rich young man who had rejected it.

Zacchaeus would have been as amazed as the other people in the crowd when Jesus stopped and asked himself over to his house. To enter someone's house in those days was the same as accepting them as they were. No pious Jew would have made himself unclean like this. This is part of what made Jesus' approach so different. He knew that the only way to bring about salvation was to get close to the people who needed it. Zacchaeus' response to Jesus' presence was repentance. He told the crowd he would return four times as much as he had stolen from them. This was the requirement laid down by the law in cases of theft. Then he went further, and it is this that shows Zacchaeus to be both truly sorry and truly trusting of Jesus' word that he was saved and welcome in God's kingdom. Without any legal obligation, Zacchaeus gave half his possessions to the poor. He had always been a descendant of Abraham by blood but now he was a descendant by faith – 'Today salvation has come to this house.'

Jesus

Jesus calls himself the **Son of Man** (in this story – 'The Son of Man came to seek and to save the lost.'). His use of this title identifies him with all the people. His task was to represent them to God and to prepare them for his kingdom. He knew their weaknesses and their sufferings and he worked with them to bring about their salvation. 'The lost' refers to everyone who is not in God's kingdom, who has turned away from the law given by Moses. The religious leaders could not accept a sinner back until he had made sacrifices in the temple, made up for what he had done wrong, and gone back to keeping the whole law. Jesus, on the other hand, accepted sinners first and gave them the opportunity to repent. Their response either led towards God or away from him, but the initiative was God's.

Bringing someone back into the Kingdom of God was more important to Jesus than being ceremonially clean. He was not afraid of the opinion of the religious leaders and disregarded the exclamations of horror when he went to Zacchaeus' house.

The excited crowds hoped Jesus was their Messiah who would bring about social and political reform but Jesus knew that the only way to lasting change was by encouraging people to change their hearts. The rest would follow one day but until human nature was brought back in line with God's original plan (see Genesis 1 and 2, pages 6–7), individual people like Zacchaeus were his priority.

> **Son of Man** – this title identifies Jesus with human suffering. He is the perfect example of how God's will can be carried out by human beings in the world.

What do you understand? **AO2**

1. Why were tax collectors hated?
2. Explain why the people were shocked when Jesus went to Zacchaeus' house.
3. What does the story teach about human nature?
4. Who does Jesus mean by 'the lost'?
5. How did Zacchaeus show his faith in Jesus?
6. How was Jesus' attitude to sinners different from that of the religious leaders?
7. Explain what Jesus meant when he said, 'Today salvation has come to this house.'
8. Why does Jesus refer to himself as the 'Son of Man'?

Essay practice

'If we change society for the better, people will also change for the better.' Do you agree? Give reasons for your answer. Show that you have considered more than one point of view.

Theology in action – seeking the lost in today's world: the work of the Salvation Army

Jesus accepted Zacchaeus just as he was. He did not judge him. He did not wait until he had changed his life. This is how he expects his followers to behave and there are many charities that do just that. The Salvation Army is one. It runs projects that help people to rediscover their self-respect and many of them also find faith in God. These three stories are adapted from their website, www.salvationarmy.org.uk.

Helping the homeless

The Salvation Army helps homeless people by providing food and shelter for those who live on the streets. The aim is not just to give them somewhere to sleep but to help them face and overcome the problems that put them on the streets in the first place. By being offered this kind of help, homeless people can start to build new lives for themselves. One person who has been helped by the Salvation Army said, 'Thank you for accepting who I am.'

Alex's story

'I'm sixteen and was homeless when the Salvation Army gave me a place in a Lifehouse centre for homeless young people. I've been there three months and it's alright. The best thing is feeling safe, away from gangs and fights. The staff are really nice and help me with college where I am doing a diploma. I've learnt a lot being here especially in the life skills classes where we discuss important issues such as sexual health and budgeting. I've even learnt to cook and can communicate with people better. My ambition now is to be a pilot. The Salvation Army turned my life around'.

Helping people affected by drug and alcohol misuse

The Salvation Army helps addicts to overcome their initial addiction and re-establishes them into the community and into their families. It runs rehabilitation centres and supports the families of the people it helps.

John's story

'My name is John and I was a heavy drinker. I drank to get drunk. I got into fights and started gambling. It is weird that something as superficial as alcohol can ruin your life. I became homeless and started to go to the Salvation Army's soup kitchen at night for a hot meal. My whole life changed when I started attending the New Futures workshop. The love, care and time they lavished on me was amazing.

I studied some of the subjects I missed at school. I made new friends and started going to Salvation Army services on Sundays. One Sunday I gave my life to God and asked him to help me with my alcohol addiction'.

Helping people who have been in prison

Many prisons in the UK have Salvation Army chaplains who visit prisoners and help them get started in life once they are released. Their ministry is practical and non-judgemental. The Salvation Army also supports the families of people they help in prison.

Paul's story

'After I had been in the prison about a week, a Salvation Army officer opened my cell door and said my mother had asked him to visit me. He never tried to preach to me, although he knew when to just talk and when to pray with me. That was over six years ago. Today I live a quiet life; I have found peace at last'.

What do you think? | AO3

1 Who are the Zacchaeuses of this day and age?
2 Why should Christians in particular help such people?

Activity

Research the work of the Salvation Army or a similar organisation.

2.5d The rich young man: Mark 10.17–27

Starter

Should the concept of a wealthy Christian be a contradiction in terms?

17 As Jesus started on his way, a man ran up to him and fell on his knees before him. 'Good teacher,' he asked, 'what must I do to inherit eternal life?'

18 'Why do you call me good?' Jesus answered. 'No one is good – except God alone. 19 You know the commandments: "You shall not murder, you shall not commit adultery, you shall not steal, you shall not give false testimony, you shall not defraud, honour your father and mother."'

20 'Teacher,' he declared, 'all these I have kept since I was a boy.'

21 Jesus looked at him and loved him. 'One thing you lack,' he said. 'Go, sell everything you have and give to the poor, and you will have treasure in heaven. Then come, follow me.'

22 At this the man's face fell. He went away sad, because he had great wealth.

23 Jesus looked around and said to his disciples, 'How hard it is for the rich to enter the Kingdom of God!'

24 The disciples were amazed at his words. But Jesus said again, 'Children, how hard it is to enter the Kingdom of God! 25 It is easier for a camel to go through the eye of a needle than for someone who is rich to enter the Kingdom of God.'

26 The disciples were even more amazed, and said to each other, 'Who then can be saved?'

27 Jesus looked at them and said, 'With man this is impossible, but not with God; all things are possible with God.'

Mark 10.17–27

Activity

Write a play about this story either to read out loud as a podcast or to be acted out on stage.

Understanding the story of the rich young man

Background to the story

Being rich in first-century Israel was seen as a sign that God had blessed you. It was a reward for the efforts you were making and the life you were leading. Most of the religious leaders were wealthy and had a high standard of living, which reinforced the belief. If you were wealthy you thought it would be easier to get into heaven. It was also a status symbol and the rich young man probably had the equivalent of a yacht in the Bahamas and a private jet. This story highlights both the kind of response to God that Jesus was looking for, and the worldly priorities that characterise human behaviour. God demands that people help to create a just world and he is on the side of the poor who are so often the victims of injustice and oppression. Did the rich young man understand and share God's passion for justice towards the poor enough to put it into practice? Unfortunately not.

The rich young man

The man was exactly the kind of enthusiastic person Jesus liked. He was a devout Jew, who kept the law, not out of a sense of duty like many others, but because he wanted to be close to God. His approach to Jesus was an emotional one and so Jesus stopped him short by asking why he had called him 'good'. The man had to recognise that he was dealing with the reality of God, not some sort of fashionable religious experience – 'no one is good – except God' said Jesus. When he asked the question, 'What must I do to inherit eternal life?' the young man expected Jesus to say, 'Well done, my friend, you've got that sorted' and he brushed aside Jesus' answer that he should keep the commandments, thinking that he scored ten out of ten on that front. But he had not understood anything about what lay behind the commandments, namely the need for active justice in the world. The Bible calls it '**righteousness**'. The law was only ever a means to an end. So when Jesus told him to give away the wealth he saw as God's favour and which was his buffer against the uncertainties of life, he was not prepared to make the sacrifice.

The disciples

They were shocked when Jesus turned the young man away. If a devout wealthy man failed the test what chance had they, poor men mostly and not nearly as knowledgeable about the law as the young man? Being rich, said Jesus, far from being a blessing, was a handicap on the road to the Kingdom of God. He said it was easier for a camel to get through the eye of a needle! He then reminded them that where human beings fail, God has the power to overcome even the most challenging situations. He said that everything was possible if they allowed God to act in their lives.

What do you understand? AO2

1 What did it mean to be rich at the time of Jesus?

2 What does the story teach about what God requires from his followers?

3 What kind of person was the rich young man? Make sure you back up your answer with evidence from the text.

4 Explain why the rich young man did not become one of Jesus' disciples.

5 Explain why the disciples were shocked when Jesus said it was easier for a camel to go through the eye of a needle than for a rich man to enter the Kingdom of God.

6 Explain what Jesus meant when he said 'all things are possible with God.'

Theology in action – rich Christians in an unequal world?

▲ A homeless man in the centre of London's financial district.

A big question today is whether it is all right for a Christian to be rich when so much of the world is poor. There seem to be three options for rich Christians: to give away all they have and become poor, to stay rich and give to deserving charities from time to time, or to develop a spirit of generosity, simple lifestyle and contentment. Jesus' disciples and Jesus himself gave up everything but he did not ask it of all who followed him. For example, Zacchaeus, the wealthy tax collector, returned what he had stolen and gave half his possessions to the poor. Presumably he kept the other half. The early Church shared everything and made sure that no one in their community was without food or shelter but this was a voluntary thing and no one was forced to give.

Some Christians justify staying rich in much the same way as people in first-century Israel did – it was God's blessing and reward, a sign of his favour. The rich young man in the story falls into this category. Christians might also say that world poverty is the fault of corrupt governments or of the poor themselves, and giving to them merely subsidises them and encourages the status quo.

Jesus was concerned with justice and he recognised a lack of it in the rich young man, who was not prepared to help the poor beyond what was demanded by the law. Many rich Christians use their wealth to combat poverty through business opportunities or charitable enterprises or giving generously to organisations at times of need. They live simply and they are content without the trappings and status symbols of their wealth.

What do you think? AO3

1 What are the options facing wealthy Christians today?

2 Which option would you take and why?

Summary of Topic 2: Human responses to God

Drawing it all together ...

This topic has been about the way human beings respond to God in different circumstances. The way they do tells us a lot about human nature – both good and bad. The stories show that people can be selfish and generous, cowardly and brave, arrogant and humble. They show that people can be faithful to God and to themselves even at great personal cost. In the Old Testament stories, people responded directly to God's word and in the New Testament, they responded to Jesus' teaching. Some people do not appear in a very good light. Adam and Eve had a perfect world but rejected God's authority, preferring to go their own way. Cain gave in to anger and jealousy with tragic results. David abused his power for his own selfish desires, and the rich young man in the last story set too much store by his possessions.

On the other hand, there are plenty of examples of people who heard God's word and put it into action. Abraham was prepared to give God what was most precious to him and learnt an important truth about God. Uriah refused to compromise his principles. Nathan delivered a hard message to his king as God had asked. Peter set aside his expectations of life to follow Jesus. Zacchaeus completely turned his life around when he met Jesus. The Roman centurion responded to Jesus with an unexpected degree of faith.

Starter

If you were to sum up the character of Jesus in three words from the stories in Topic 2, which three words would you choose?

Discuss

Discuss the following questions and write a response to them.

1 Which characters do you think had the most faith? Choose the top five and explain why you have selected them.

2 Out of all the characters you have met, who ranks as the worst? Explain why you think he or she is worse than the others.

3 Who impresses you most?

4 Who would you most like to meet and why?

5 Who would you least like to meet and why?

Collate the opinions of everyone in the class and create a graph to show the most popular choices.

Activity

Look at the box on the right. Match each character on the left with one or more characteristic on the right. There will be a lot of overlap! Create a diagram to show the range of responses the characters had to God, both directly and through Jesus. You may add more characteristics to the right-hand column if you want to.

Character	Characteristic – people who ...
Adam	were faithful
Eve	were disobedient
Cain	were powerful
Abel	listened out for God
Abraham	were courageous
David	had integrity
Bathsheba	were obedient
Uriah	said sorry
Nathan	misused their position
Peter	were prepared to make sacrifices
Zacchaeus	were grateful to God
The centurion	were obedient to the law
The rich young man	were selfish
The Pharisees	were victims of the sin of others

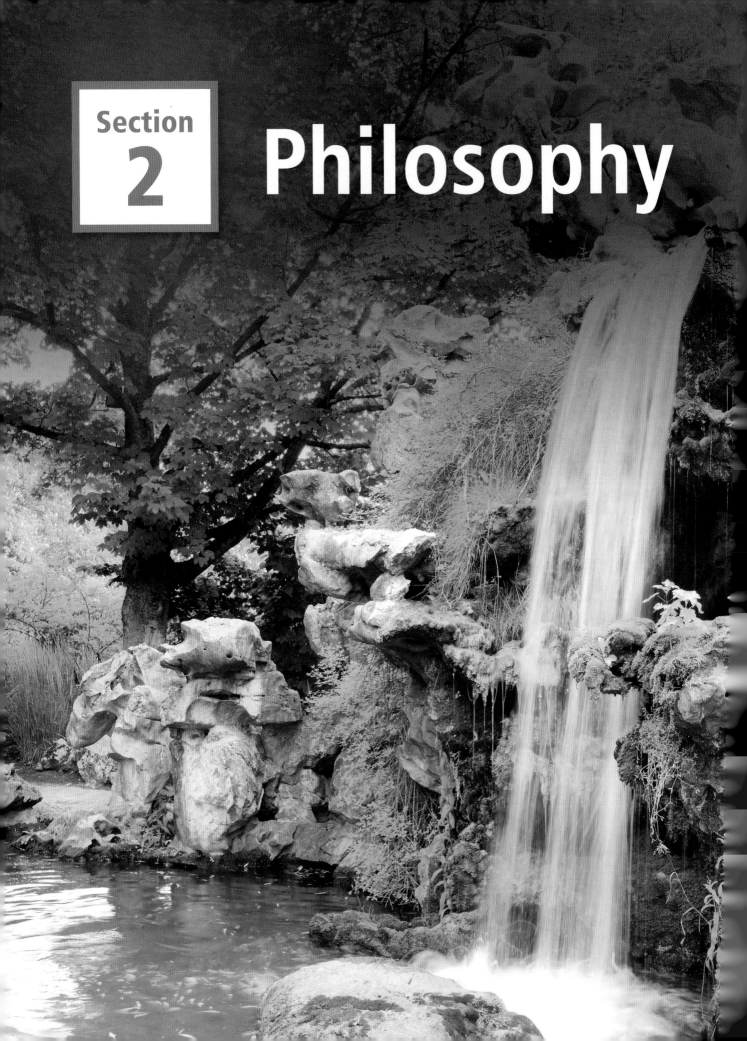

Section 2 Philosophy

What is philosophy?

The word 'philosophy' literally means 'the love of wisdom'. The word is taken from two Greek words: *philos* (love) and *sophos* (wisdom). Wisdom is the human desire to understand the world as it actually is and, by knowing this, to live a more fulfilled life.

Starter

What is a persuasive argument?

▲ Socrates said that the purpose of philosophy was to question everything. Without philosophy, he said, 'The unexamined life is not worth living'.

Truth claims

Philosophers are not content with being told that something is true, they want to know *why* it is true (or false) and the means by which this truth has been established. Philosophers point out that there are lots of different *kinds* of **truth claims** and it is important to sort these out, otherwise one kind of truth might be confused with another kind and then we won't know what is *really* true and what is *really* false.

For example, consider the following truth claims:

- London is the capital of the United Kingdom.
- God is all-powerful.
- The First World War was caused by the assassination of Archduke Franz Ferdinand.
- Humans are mammals.
- 7 + 5 = 12

None of these truth claims is particularly controversial. London is the capital of the UK is a political truth claim; God is all-powerful is a theological truth claim; the cause of the First World War is a historical truth claim; humans are mammals is a biological truth claim; 7 + 5 = 12 is a mathematical truth claim.

Some of these truth claims might be **disputed**. Some might argue about what is *meant* by saying God is all-powerful; some might argue that the assassination was a *probable* cause but not a direct cause of the First World War; a Scottish nationalist might *not recognise* London as being the capital of the United Kingdom but only England; some might argue that claiming humans are mammals is *insufficient* because there are other characteristics which must be included.

The role of philosophy is to make **clear** what the problems are. This is often a complex and sometimes very technical process. The philosopher's job is to point out where beliefs and arguments have become confused because a belief may assume certain things which are false or an argument may have used the wrong method of reasoning.

To analyse arguments, philosophers have developed many special methods and techniques. We will now look at some which you will find useful when you are analysing other people's arguments and constructing your own.

What do you know? — AO1

1 What does the word 'philosophy' mean?
2 Give an example of a historical truth claim.
3 Give an example of a theological truth claim.

What do you understand? — AO2

4 Explain what a truth claim is.
5 Explain what it means to dispute a truth claim.
6 Explain the main purpose of philosophy.

Philosophers' methods

Validity and soundness

An argument is a series of connected statements (or premises) ending with a conclusion (or proposition).

● For an argument to be **valid**, each statement made has to be logically linked or connected to the conclusion.

● For an argument to be **sound**, each statement also has to be actually true.

This can be confusing because an argument can be logically valid even if the statements are false. For example:

● Everyone who reads a Harry Potter book is a genius.

● Mary is reading a Harry Potter book.

● So, Mary is a genius.

Logically, the argument is valid even though the first statement is not *actually* true. The argument is valid because the conclusion contains *only* the truth claims of each of the two previous statements. You might note that when you come to write an essay, your conclusion (at the end of the essay) should *never* add a new idea.

A sound argument is one where the statements are *actually* true. For example:

● All pupils at this school wear blue ties.

● Harry is a pupil at this school.

● So, Harry wears a blue tie.

The argument is valid and sound. It is valid because the conclusion contains the truth claims of the two statements; it is sound because the two truth claims are actually true (Harry is indeed a pupil at this school).

Now you know how a valid and sound argument works, you are in a position to **refute** or reject an argument by pointing out where its reasoning has gone wrong.

Activity
1 Make up an argument which is valid but not sound.
2 Share your example with someone in your class or group and ask them to explain why the argument is valid but not sound.
3 Now make up a sound argument and share it with someone in your class or group. Ask them to give reasons why they think the argument is valid and sound.

▲ 'Police help dog bite victim.' Be careful of ambiguity when making arguments!

Tools to analyse arguments

Here are some things to look out for which may make an argument invalid or unsound:

● **False statements**. Statements that can be disputed because they are factually unlikely or incorrect weaken the validity of an argument and make it unsound. For example, an argument based on the fact that whales are fish is faulty because whales are, in fact, mammals.

● **Ambiguity and definitions**. Words often have more than one meaning. An argument is weakened when it includes a word or phrase that has a number of different meanings. For example, 'Police help dog bite victim' could mean that the police encouraged the dog to bite the victim or that the police were helping a person who had been bitten by a dog. Many arguments rely on definitions, but some definitions are too general, too narrow or inaccurate. For example, I might use the word 'mankind' to refer to all male humans, when it usually refers to all people. On the other hand, if I define wrongdoing as anything that causes pain, then this too broad a definition as a surgeon might cause pain but will not be doing wrong.

● **Contradictions**. A very basic philosophical rule is that a statement cannot be true and false at the same time. For example, either I exist or I do not exist; I cannot exist and not exist at the same time. If I claim that I do indeed exist and not exist at the same time then I have contradicted myself. This principle is known as the **law of non-contradiction**.

● **Analogies**. It is very common in argument to use something that is known to explain something new. A good analogy must have as many points of similarity as possible with that which it is comparing itself to. For example, **Jesus** used parables or analogies of everyday life to teach others. In the Parable of the Good Samaritan, he used a story to answer a question. **Plato**'s most famous parable is that of the cave, which he used to explain the philosophical journey to discover the difference between illusion and reality. (See page 101 for more about Plato's parable of the cave.) A poor or **weak analogy** is where there are only a few points of contact between the things being compared, or where there are many irrelevancies. **David Hume** attacked the design argument for God's existence because he considered it was based on a weak analogy. (See pages 105–108 for more about Hume's criticisms of the analogy of design and God's existence.)

What do you know? AO1

1 What is a false statement?

2 What is the principle of non-contradiction?

What do you understand? AO2

3 Explain what it means to refute an argument.

4 Give an example of a word that has more than one meaning. Explain its various meanings.

Different areas of philosophy

As philosophy is interested in the basic truths about the world, over time philosophers have developed distinct areas of philosophy. Traditionally the questions that philosophers have asked and tried to answer are:

- What can I know and how do I know it is true? This is called **epistemology.**

- What is real and how does it exist? This is called **metaphysics.**

- What ought I to do? This is called moral philosophy or **ethics.**

- What is a valid argument? This is called **logic.**

A fifth area is the **history of philosophy.** Although this area of philosophy doesn't have a central question which it is attempting to answer, it is important that we understand when ideas developed and influenced each other. Quite often when we study a particular philosopher we need to know what was going on at the time to make sense of the questions and answers the philosopher was interested in.

In this course you are going to study four western philosophers. You will need to know the historical context in which they were living and the central ideas that occupied their thoughts. Of course, there are thousands more philosophers and ideas you could study; this course is just a start.

- Protagoras (c. 490–c. 420 BC)
- **Plato (428/427–348/347 BC)***
- Aristotle (384–322 BC)
- Cicero (106–43 BC)
- Augustine (354–430)
- Anselm (c. 1033–1109)
- Aquinas (1225–1274)
- Erasmus (1466–1536)
- Descartes (1596–1650)
- Locke (1632–1704)
- Leibniz (1646–1716)
- **Hume (1711–1776)***
- Kant (1724–1804)
- Hegel (1770–1831)
- **Mill (1806–1873)***
- Wittgenstein (1889–1951)
- Sartre (1905–1980)
- **King (1929– 1968)***

* Philosophers in bold are studied in this course

Activity
Find out about one of the philosophers and present your findings to the class. Don't choose one of the philosophers marked *.

Essay practice
'Philosophy is the most important subject there is to study.' Do you agree? Give reasons for your answer. Show that you have considered more than one point of view.

Topic 1

Great thinkers and their ideas

→ ## 1.1 Plato's life and thought

Plato's life

Starter
How do we know that what we believe is really true?

We don't know much about the early life of Plato (427–347BC) except that he came from an aristocratic family and lived in ancient Athens during a period of great turmoil mostly caused by the Peloponnesian War (431–404BC). Many Athenians hoped for a return to better times. Among those who argued for a new form of democracy were Socrates (who died in 399BC) and his pupil Plato. Plato is often regarded as the founder of Western philosophy. The conversation below will help you understand his life and thought.

Imaginary dialogue between Plato and his brother Glaucon

The year is 386BC. Plato has just returned from Syracuse, Sicily, where he has been tutoring King Dionysius I's son. He and his eldest brother Glaucon, also a philosopher, are inside the Temple of Athena in Athens.

▲ The Temple of Athena in Athens.

▲ Plato

Glaucon: It is very good to see you, brother. Your brother Adeimantus and I have greatly missed you, for it is now just over ten years since you left Athens after the death of our great friend and philosopher Socrates, and we have much to discuss. How was your stay in Syracuse?

Plato: To be honest, Glaucon, it was a failure. I had hoped to teach the king's son to think philosophically, as Socrates taught us, but he had hated mathematics and couldn't see how this would be of any use when he became a ruler. So, after a year, I decided to return home.

Glaucon: Well, I am very pleased you have because now you can resume your role in politics and guide Athens back into democracy. Perhaps we can return to the golden days when Athens was truly great. You have spent the last ten years as a soldier, fought three campaigns, travelled widely, and are a respected philosopher; you are practical, experienced and wise. You owe it to Athens to be a politician.

Plato: Glaucon, do you remember nothing Socrates taught us? The point he was constantly making was that politicians and rulers only want power, when what they should be doing is debating about what true justice is, what goodness is and what is meant by fairness. *Then* there is hope that Athens can be ruled wisely and democratically for all.

Glaucon: This is all very well, but Socrates could be a bit abstract. Of course it is all about power. Since the unfortunate death of Pericles (429BC) Athens has lived through an **oligarchy** (rule by a few people over many people). If you remember, our mother's uncle and cousin were oligarchs but that ended in bloodshed. **Democracy** (rule by many people) only works when those who rule know what to do with power. As we know, to our cost, our democratic rulers haven't all been well educated to deal with it properly.

Plato: Precisely, Glaucon! Education is the key to it all. That's why I have returned to Athens to set up a university called the Academy, to educate our future leaders. When I was growing up and being prepared to become a political leader all that mattered was that one could speak well in public by giving clever speeches.

Glaucon: Are you referring to the teaching of the Sophists?

Plato: I am. The Sophist philosophers have become very popular among rich Greek families because they think that with a Sophist education they can get influential positions in government. They are not all bad. I remember, as if it were yesterday, a formidable debate between Socrates and Protagoras, the leading Sophist. Even though Protagoras' arguments were clever, Socrates showed brilliantly that there has to be more to philosophy than merely winning arguments.

Glaucon: That sounds very odd – surely that is its purpose?

Plato: No! What matters is that you are forced to think beyond the obvious to the way things really are. That is why Socrates was seen as a threat to democracy. To the new democrats, Socrates' method of questioning everything and forcing the young men of Athens to think for themselves was seen as a rejection of the gods (impiety) and the traditions of Athens (treason). At his trial he described himself like a horsefly; a horsefly stings people and stirs us up. That's what Socrates sees philosophy as doing – stinging people into awareness by making them ask questions. Again, at his trial Socrates defended his teaching and said that without philosophy 'the unexamined life is not worth living'.

Glaucon: I think I can see where you are going with your plan for the Academy. You want to teach our young men to be skilful thinkers and not just be clever show-offs.

Plato: That's right. As young aristocrats, we were taught in the traditional Greek way to read the works of our great poets, such as Homer, and to learn to imitate the gods and heroes of our past. This was good because we need good moral role models, but we have to go further. The skilful thinker has to want to know what is the very *best and perfect form* of goodness and justice.

Glaucon: And, presumably, only your philosopher rulers or kings will know this?

Plato: Yes, because as only the philosopher rulers will know real goodness from illusory goodness, they are the only ones who are able to rule *everyone* fairly and justly. Socrates hinted at this, but his questions only focused on morality. I want to go much further and think about what is absolutely real and true. When I was in Syracuse last year I spoke with the **Pythagorean** philosophers. They helped me realise that mathematics shows us that everything in this world is not perfect and is only a reflection of a perfect reality.

Glaucon: Let me see if I have understood you correctly. If I draw a circle I know it will never be absolutely perfect even though I know mathematically there is such a thing as a perfect circle. I wouldn't know it was imperfect unless there *actually* existed a perfect circle.

Plato: Glaucon, I can see that at this rate you will be one of my top students at the Academy!

Glaucon: Maybe, but I can also see now why young Dionysius found your tutoring rather abstract and irrelevant.

Plato: You are right; we have jumped in at the most advanced and abstract stage. I am writing a book, *The Republic*, which will guide Academy students over several years. The chapter I am writing at the moment is all about the philosopher ruler, but the chapter before was about the family and the role of women in society.

Glaucon: I hope your book won't be too abstract and dry.

Plato: Well, as it happens, in the chapter I am writing I have presented three stories or allegories. The first is called The Sun, the second The Divided Line and the third is called The Cave. You need to read all three of them together, but The Cave summarises why we need philosophy education and why being a philosopher is not intellectually and emotionally easy.

Glaucon: Why is it not emotionally easy?

Plato: Because there is the risk that philosophy will question everything you believe, and you may find out that a lot of what you thought was true is false.

Glaucon: But isn't that what it means to live the 'examined life'?

Plato: That's right, Glaucon. (*They step out of the Temple of Athena into the dazzling sunshine.*) At the moment, you can't see, and your eyes hurt because the sun is too bright. But you will soon get used to it. That is what philosophy is like. (*They walk slowly to the bottom of the temple steps in silence.*) Thank you, brother, for our discussion – it has given me an idea. I'm going to make you one of the key characters in my book in dialogue with Socrates in the same manner as we have discussed matters today. Socrates was a master of the philosophical dialogue; he strongly criticised the Sophists for talking too much and failing to question and debate ideas.

Glaucon: I am flattered.

Plato: You should be!

What do you know?

1 Outline what Socrates taught.
2 Outline four key events in Plato's life.
3 What is the role of the philosopher kings?
4 Who were the Sophists?

What do you understand?
AO2

5 Explain the purpose of Plato's Academy.
6 Explain the difference between oligarchy and democracy.

The Parable of the Cave

The Parable or Allegory of the Cave is one of three stories Plato tells to explain his theory that there is a reality greater than our experience of this world. It is also a story about the journey the philosopher makes from having to give up their ordinary ignorant beliefs about this world to discover the world of reality.

The following is a summary of the story Socrates relates to Glaucon in *The Republic*.

The chamber, shadows and the prisoners

Imagine there is an underground cave with a long tunnel to the entrance and daylight. The entrance is as wide as the cave itself. In the chamber of the cave there are people who have been held prisoner there since they were children. Their legs and necks are fastened so they can only look about the chamber of the cave and not towards its entrance.

Now near the entrance of the cave, and out of sight from the prisoners, there is a fire burning. In front of the fire there is a road and a wall running alongside the road. All kinds of objects and creatures move up and down the road but because of the wall, the prisoners can't see the actual objects and creatures. Because of the fire, however, the shadows of these objects and creatures are projected down into the chamber onto the cave wall. The prisoners of course treat these shadows as real objects and creatures – even their sounds and voices appear real. The prisoners believe that these shadows are the whole truth of reality.

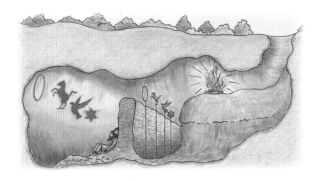

The journey of the released prisoner and the sun

Now imagine, one day, a prisoner has his chains removed and is made to stand up, turn his head from the wall of the cave and to look at and then walk towards the fire. He would find all these actions very painful, and his eyes especially would be dazzled by the light from the fire. But he would also realise that what he believed before about the world was all wrong. He might even want to return to the cave where life was less painful, and he could see properly without being dazzled – where the shadows seemed more real than this new experience.

But, then imagine he is dragged up the steep path to the mouth of the cave and then into the sunlight. Although this also would be painful, he would become convinced that this was reality, and the shadows in the cave were not real. Gradually, he would see the light of the sun reflected off objects. Then, as his eyes became used to this, he would be able to look directly at the sun.

Our ex-prisoner would now be very pleased to have this new knowledge and would regard his life in the cave as meaningless by comparison.

The return of the ex-prisoner to the cave

Imagine now our ex-prisoner returns to the cave. At first, his eyes would not be adjusted to the dark and while he was getting used to seeing in the dark again, the prisoners would think that his journey had been a waste of time and that he had been a fool to make it. Imagine that he tried to teach the prisoners the truth of what he had discovered, so that they too might be set free. How do you think they would react?

Why, they would be angry with him and try and kill him.

Activity
Read the Parable of the Cave carefully and then make a storyboard to illustrate the journey of the prisoner.

Discuss

Why is the ex-prisoner treated so badly when he returns to the cave?

Understanding the Parable of the Cave

The Parable of the Cave may be interpreted in many different ways. Here are some interpretations of its key symbols:

- **Prisoners**. The prisoners represent how most ordinary people believe what they have been brought up to believe, without thinking carefully about whether the things they believe are actually true. Their minds are in a state of illusion.

- **Shadows**. The shadows represent the world as it appears to most people. The symbol of the shadows suggests that we are not seeing the world as it really is, but the version that we have been led to believe exists. It is as if we are watching a film and believing that what we see on the screen is actually happening.

- **The journey out of the cave**. The story doesn't tell us who releases the chains from one of the prisoners and makes him climb towards the entrance of the cave, but Plato later suggests that this occurs when people go to school and start to think for themselves. The journey is the journey of the mind from ignorance to true knowledge. It is hard work; learning how to think philosophically is a painful process.

- **Sun**. Plato tells us that the sun represents the source of truth, in the same way that the sun is the source of life and light. The sun is ultimate reality. Plato calls this ultimate reality 'the Good'. The Good is known through reason, not belief.

- **Reaction of the prisoners**. The return of the ex-prisoner illustrates how difficult it is for the philosopher to explain philosophical ideas to those who are ignorant of philosophy or find it threatening. This encourages philosophers to be generous with their new knowledge and adapt it skilfully to the ordinary world. There is a warning; those philosophers who provoke the world too much risk losing their lives.

What do you understand? AO2

1 Explain why Plato uses the idea of shadows to explain our experience of the world.

2 Explain why the prisoner has to be forced to turn round and leave the cave.

3 Explain what the sun represents. Give some examples.

4 Explain why the ex-prisoner found it difficult to return to the cave.

Essay practice

'The most important thing in life is education.' Do you agree? Give reasons for your answer. Show that you have considered more than one point of view.

What do you think? AO3

5 Imagine you could choose a virtual reality program so you could live a life that fulfilled all your desires and made you very happy. Would this actually be better than living in the real world? Why?

6 Is it worth seeking the truth if it makes you unhappy?

1.2 David Hume's life and thought

David Hume's life

David Hume (1711–76) was brought up in Scotland but travelled widely in Europe. He is regarded as one of the most influential philosophers today. Hume's aim was to apply the scientific discoveries of Newton to philosophy; this made him question traditional views of religion and ethics. The following conversation will help you understand his life and thought.

An imaginary conversation between David Hume and Adam Smith

The year is 1776 and David Hume is in the drawing room of his home in St Andrew's Square, New Town, Edinburgh. He is not well, but he is in very good spirits and is in deep conversation with his friend, the philosopher Adam Smith. During the conversation he has many visitors, but his doctor, Dr Black, turns them away.

Starter
Can God's existence be proved?

▲ Hume

Hume: I have to be frank with you, Adam, I don't think these stomach pains of mine will go away. I know that I probably haven't long to live. This will be my last conversation with you – I want you to remember me as I have always been throughout my life, as a happy, optimistic and sociable person.

Smith: You have certainly been that, for although you have faced strong criticism for your challenges to Christian beliefs, you have always remained positive; it hasn't stopped you from pursuing your philosophical writings. Looking back, do you think you have been a success as an author?

Hume: All I wanted – even as an eighteen-year-old – was to be admired as a writer; this has been the driving force throughout my adult life. But it has been far from easy. My first book, *A Treatise of Human Nature*, was published in 1739 when I was 25, but was severely criticised for being unclear. In many ways I regret writing it now, but it launched me into philosophical research and taught me that I had to be careful not to make my new and radical ideas too extreme.

Smith: You seem to have had these radical ideas at an early age. Was that a result of your upbringing?

Hume: Well, as you know, although some of my family were aristocratic and my father a successful lawyer; his death in 1713, two years after my birth, meant that my mother was not especially

wealthy. I am now a wealthy man, but that has been the result of my own career. It was clear to my family that I was a clever child and a good career for me would have been to follow in my father's footsteps and become a lawyer. So, I was sent at the very young age of twelve to Edinburgh University to study law. I hated it, but then I came across a number of philosophers who were part of what I call the **'new scene of thought'**.

Smith: Yes, they were the radical philosophers who were questioning religion and looking for a scientific basis of knowledge, morals, economics and politics.

Hume: That's right. I could see immediately that Sir Isaac Newton's scientific discoveries challenged so many beliefs. These beliefs, which we have held for centuries, are almost certainly wrong because they are not based on reason and experience, which can be tested and demonstrated to be true.

Smith: Can you give me a simple example?

Hume: Of course. Many people think that there are moral laws, just like the laws of nature, which tell us, for example, that it is wrong to murder and the right to marry. But when we think about it carefully, these laws are not laws of nature at all, but just feelings that we share with each other and treat *as if* they are laws. I would even argue that there are no moral facts!

Smith: I can't imagine our Church leaders being very impressed with your views.

Hume: Indeed. The Church ministers have accused me of being an **atheist** and an **infidel**. They successfully petitioned the authorities not to make me professor of moral philosophy at Edinburgh University in 1742 and Glasgow University in 1752. Do you know that in 1756 the Church of Scotland even tried to **excommunicate** me? They didn't succeed.

Smith: Are you an atheist? How would you describe your philosophical position?

Hume: It depends on what you think God is. I do not believe in God in any traditional sense, although I accept that there may be an underlying principle of the universe. I am a **sceptic**; that means that I believe that many things we hold to be true are not so when you test them scientifically and through reason.

Smith: So, as you did not become a university professor, how have you managed to support yourself as a philosopher?

Hume: I have had an interesting and varied career. In 1734 I tried my hand at banking in Bristol. This earned me enough money to travel to France where I wrote my first book in 1739. Even though it was not a success I made enough money to write my next book in 1742, which was much better received. After a dreadful year tutoring the Marquess of Annandale. I then became secretary to General St Clair.

Smith: But this can't have been the source of your wealth today?

Hume: No, this came about unexpectedly through my bestseller, *The History of England*, which was published in six volumes over several years – the last volume coming out in 1762. The other job I enjoyed was as secretary to Lord Hertford when he was British Ambassador to Paris. In Paris I mixed with a group of philosophers called *Les Philosophes*, who much admired my ideas.

Smith: And, if I recall correctly, you were then honoured by being appointed Under Secretary of State, Northern Department in 1767 and based in London?

Hume: Yes, I did this for a year before returning to Edinburgh. I was 58 and wanted more time to revise my earlier philosophical publications.

Smith: Such as your two highly influential books *An Enquiry Concerning Human Nature* and *An Enquiry Concerning the Principles of Morals*. Presumably, both books continue to develop your sceptical reasoning?

Hume: Yes, that's right. Although I think we should test all beliefs about the world scientifically. I have come to the conclusion that cause and effect don't actually exist in nature!

Smith: Don't get over excited, David, otherwise Dr Black will send me home.

Hume: Quite so. (*He calms down.*) Adam, old friend, thank you for visiting. I have had a wonderful life; I don't fear death as I don't believe we have an immortal soul, but I would like to live longer so I can write more. However, yesterday I had an imaginary conversation in my mind with Charon – the boatman in Greek mythology who transported the dead to the underworld – and asked him for a little more time on Earth to produce a new edition of one of my books. Charon replied, 'But if you make some corrections you will want more time to make more. Get into the boat this instant, you lazy loitering rogue!'

(*Hume falls into thoughtful silence. Smith takes this as his cue to leave. Dr Black sees him out.*)

What do you know? AO1

1 Outline Hume's early life up to his time in Bristol.
2 How did the 'new scene of thought' change Hume's way of thinking?
3 Name three of Hume's most influential books on philosophy.

What do you understand? AO2

4 Explain why Hume was accused of being an 'infidel'.
5 Explain how Hume's religious scepticism affected his career negatively.

Arguments for God's existence and Hume's objections

Even though the many arguments for the existence of God may not prove God's existence, they raise fundamental issues about the nature of the world and its meaning.

What kind of proof would convince you that God exists? For thousands of years the answer to this question has been that the world is too organised, purposeful and beautiful to suggest that it is here by chance, and that it must be the result of a creative power or God.

For example, back in the sixth century BC, the prophet Isaiah wrote:

> *Lift up your eyes and look to the heavens: Who created all these? He who brings out the starry host one by one and calls forth each of them by name. Because of his great power and mighty strength, not one of them is missing.*
>
> Isaiah 40.26

For many people the fact that, as Isaiah says, the vast cosmos (the 'starry host') does not collapse but is sustained and ordered is enough to indicate that God is the creative force of the universe.

But is this experience enough to *prove* God's existence? To be a proof, this experience has to be set up as a philosophical argument. The most common philosophical argument used here is an **analogical** one.

The design argument for God's existence uses analogy. The philosophical debate is whether the analogies are good ones.

....

analogy – a comparison of two things, where what is true of one thing (which I know directly and for certain) is true by implication of the other (which I may not know directly or for certain)

....

The design argument

There are two stages to the design argument:

- **Stage 1: the argument for design**. This stage of the argument establishes whether creation is ordered.

- **Stage 2: the argument from design**. The second stage of the argument argues that if there is order, then it must have been designed by a designer, and as that designer must be all-powerful to create a universe, then this designer is God.

The argument for design

The phrase 'for design' is slightly misleading: what is really meant by design is **order**. Hume argues that there are very few people who would deny that there is some kind of order in the universe. If there were no order, then things would collapse very quickly. Everywhere one looks there is order – from the simplest organism such as an amoeba to the eye, nature is extraordinary in its complexity and organisation.

The argument from design

This is the more complex philosophical stage of the argument. It aims to show that the order of the universe points to a higher intelligence, and that this intelligence is the all-powerful (omnipotent), all-knowing (omniscient) and all-loving (omnibenevolent) God that Christians, Jews and Muslims worship.

The argument uses an analogy to show why there must be a higher intelligence. Here are two of Hume's examples:

  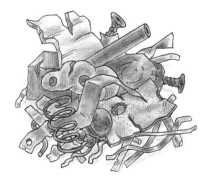 

▲ A pile of bricks has no order and purpose, but a house does. The house has been designed by an intelligent being, i.e. an architect.

▲ We know that the parts of the watch have been designed by an intelligent craftsman to create a complex object out of random metal, the purpose of which is to indicate time.

The argument from design may be summarised as follows:

1 Everywhere in the world, we observe order and purpose.

2 We know from experience of things that humans create (such as houses and watches) that order and purpose is the result of our intelligent minds.

3 Therefore, by analogy, the created world must also be the result of an intelligent mind.

4 This intelligent mind must be much greater than a human mind to create an ordered universe, so this mind must be all-powerful, all-intelligent and all-loving. We give this super intelligent mind the name God.

You may already have spotted some flaws in this argument. Hume raised many objections.

What do you understand? [AO2]

1 Explain what an analogy is.

2 Explain why a watch or a house indicates the existence of a designer.

3 Explain how, by using the analogy of a watch or a house, we might conclude the world must also have a designer (God).

What do you think? [AO3]

4 Do you think the design argument for God's existence is a good one?

Hume's objections to the design argument

Hume was intrigued by the argument from design. He never completely dismissed it but he did raise many objections to it. He sets them out in dialogue form in his book *Dialogues Concerning Natural Religion* (1779). In his will he requested the book to be published after his death because he feared that it would upset a lot of people. The three key characters in the dialogue are:

- **Cleanthes** – a philosopher who puts forward the design argument

- **Philo** – a sceptical philosopher, who raises many objections to the design argument

- **Demea** – a traditional Christian believer.

Here are some of Philo's philosophical objections:

As the world appears to be evolving, a much better analogy would be to compare it to an animal or vegetable, which develops by reproducing itself. If this is so, then there is no external super conscious intelligence who is infinite and loves the creation, just the general laws of science.

Human minds like to impose order, patterns and design on things. How can we be sure that what we see in nature really is the product of one super intelligent mind, and not our own minds imposing order?

It may be true that our part of the universe appears to be designed, but how do we know that the *whole* of the universe is designed? If we cannot be sure of this, then we cannot say that the intelligent designer is omnipotent. If he is not omnipotent, then he is not God.

Might it be that God made many very poor versions of the universe until he happened to produce this one? Perhaps it would be better to compare God to a child or weak old person than the omnipotent, perfect God, which is what the design argument is aiming to prove.

Perhaps matter just obeys its own laws and there is no grand purpose to creation. For example, when I think of an idea, the idea is created by me internally in my mind. If this is so, then there is no external 'mind' ordering the universe.

The analogy of the bricks and the single architect is flawed. How do we know that the universe is designed by one architect? Buildings often have several architects (plans could be drawn up by a firm of architects). If this is so, then the universe might have been designed by several minds. This would support **polytheism** not **monotheism**; this is not compatible with Christianity.

Here are two of Demea's Christian objections:

> All the design argument can do is point to God's existence; human minds are far too weak and feeble ever to presume to know anything about the infinite God and his nature. The only way we can know about God is through what he reveals to us through his prophets and in Jesus Christ.

> It is human arrogance to think that God is anything like the human mind. The design argument is basically flawed because of its **anthropomorphism**. Anthropomorphism means seeing the world in human terms. We often do this in stories about animals where we make them behave and even think like humans. In the design argument, the idea of God as a super intelligent mind just makes him like a super human mind, when the point is that God is totally different from the creation.

Activity

In groups, choose one of Hume's objections and give a short speech defending it. Then choose another of his objections and give a short speech saying what is wrong with it.

Essay practice

'There is so much beauty, order and purpose in the world, that it must have been designed by God.' Do you agree? Give reasons for your answer. Show that you have considered more than one point of view.

▲ Is this a random set of splodges or a dog drinking off the ground in a snow storm? What are your reasons to support your view?

1.3 John Stuart Mill's life and thought

John Stuart Mill's life

Starter
What does it mean to behave ethically?

John Stuart Mill (1806–73) was the son of the philosopher James Mill. James Mill was very keen that his son should excel academically and this led to John's nervous breakdown in his early twenties. He recovered and went on to campaign for social reforms in the nineteenth century including women's rights and the abolition of slavery. He wrote many philosophy books which still have great influence today. The following conversation will help you understand his life and thought.

An imaginary interview with John Stuart Mill and an admirer

John Stuart Mill is being interviewed in the garden of his house in Avignon, France. Mill's stepdaughter, Helen (who lives with him) brings out tea. The year is 1873; Mill would die later in the year.

▲ John Stuart Mill

Interviewer: Mr Mill, thank you for seeing me. May I say how much I have enjoyed reading your book *Autobiography*? As an admirer of all that you have written and campaigned for, it was most interesting to see how your philosophical beliefs have driven your life. Can you outline how you arrived at your basic philosophical views?

Mill: Thank you. As I look back over my life, I can safely say that there were two major influences on my philosophy: Jeremy Bentham (1748–1832) and John Austin (1750–1859). My father, James (also a philosopher), met Bentham when I was only two years old, and became a deep admirer.

Interviewer: What was it that Bentham taught that was so influential?

Mill: Bentham taught that society should be run on rational and scientific moral principles. His moral philosophy is called **utilitarianism**: a very simple idea that laws and morality should be tested, to make sure they produce the greatest happiness of the greatest number of people. If they don't, then they should be revised or abolished.

Interviewer: And so, you were taught this at the age of two?

Mill: Not quite, but my father was insistent that I learnt to think for myself from a very early age. He didn't want me indoctrinated by traditional religious beliefs, although he did expect me to think about them intelligently. So, by the age of three my father had taught me Greek and Latin, and by the age of six I had read many of the Greek classics including Plato's dialogues. My father then made me study logic and algebra when I was twelve and politics and economics at thirteen.

Interviewer: It doesn't sound as if you had time to do much else. Did you have friends?

Mill: No, I didn't. You'll remember that in my autobiography I wrote, 'I never was a boy; never played at cricket; it is better to let Nature have her way.' But I loved reading and writing poetry and studying ideas, so at the time I didn't miss friendships. I was also motivated by Bentham's powerful utilitarian idea that society could and should be reformed.

Interviewer: So, I presume, being an intellectual high-flyer, you went to Oxford or Cambridge to study – although I don't remember you mentioning this in your book.

Mill: I couldn't go to either university because my father was a **non-conformist**, and the two universities required its students to be members of the Church of England. John Austin, who was professor of law and a family friend, almost persuaded me to study law, but after a couple of years I gave this up and in 1823 took a job in the East India Company. This was well paid and also gave me time to read and write.

Interviewer: So, you had good prospects, and as a member of Bentham's utilitarian movement you were ready to help reform society?

Mill: That's right, but then suddenly in 1826, at the age of twenty, it all fell apart. I was deeply depressed and I realised that although Bentham's view of society was perhaps still worth fighting for, I no longer felt motivated to be one of his followers. It is not enough for a society simply to seek to maximise pleasures; it needs a greater vision than this.

Interviewer: How did you manage to overcome your depression? Did you give up being a utilitarian?

Mill: It was by reading the poetry of Wordsworth. His sense of the beauty of nature and how this makes human beings more compassionate to each other gave me a new vision for society. Although I stopped being a Benthamite, I adapted his ideas into my own version of utilitarianism in my book *Utilitarianism* (1863). My view is that a utilitarian society must encourage the 'higher pleasures', such as art, music, poetry and philosophy. Without these, society would be greatly diminished.

Interviewer: I have to return to London soon, but before I go, could you tell me about some of your social reforms? Perhaps, we could begin with your pioneering work for women's rights.

Mill: First I should mention that my other key book is called *On Liberty* (1859). In this book, I argued that we can't be truly happy unless we are free to make our own decisions. This is something that Bentham entirely overlooked but I think that without freedom of speech and expression we cannot be fulfilled and happy people. And that applies to *all* humans – not just men but women as well. That's what I argued in my book *The Subjection of Women* (1869). It is obvious that men and women should have the same rights, access to education, opportunity to vote and opportunities in the workplace. That's why I have been an outspoken critic of slavery of *all* kinds.

Interviewer: I agree! You are very passionate about women's rights. Is this something your mother taught you?

Mill: Not my mother, but the most important woman in my life, Harriet Taylor, whose daughter is having tea with us now. Harriet and I met in 1830 and I knew immediately that, besides being beautiful, she was witty and highly intelligent. It was she who made me revise parts of *On Liberty* and inspired me to write *The Subjection of Women*. Harriet and I were close friends for twenty years and only able to marry when her husband died in 1851. Sadly, we were only married for seven years before my dear Harriet died of tuberculosis fifteen years ago.

Interviewer: Besides your books, how were you able to bring about some of the social reforms you feel Britain so urgently needs to carry out?

Mill: In 1865, I was fortunate to be elected as Member of Parliament. I was able to speak on giving the vote to the working classes (not just people who owned property) and the **Irish problem**, and I was the first person in Westminster to argue for women's **suffrage** (the ability to vote). Although I was only an MP for three years, I enjoyed being part of the practical process of government and reform.

Interviewer: Thank you, Mr Mill. I can see why you have often been judged to be one of the greatest philosophers and political thinkers of the nineteenth century. I imagine that your influential ideas will continue to be discussed for many years to come.

What do you know? AO1

1 Outline the main events of Mill's life until he was twenty years old.
2 What was Mill's main argument in his book *Utilitarianism*?
3 Describe the reforms Mill wanted for women.
4 Name two other important books by Mill.

John Stuart Mill's teaching

What are ethics?

You hear some pupils in your year group bad-mouthing a friend of yours. Your friend asks you whether you have heard anything bad said about them.

Do you tell the truth, which would hurt their feelings considerably, or do you lie and say that you haven't heard anything?

Is it ever right to lie? The answer to this will depend on the basis of your moral decision. Here are three responses:

- A **Christian** response might be one based on the Bible. In the Ten Commandments it states that 'you shall not give false testimony against your neighbour' (Exodus 20.16). From a traditional Christian point of view, as this is God's command then it must be always wrong to lie, even for good reasons, because lying is breaking God's law and causing a breakdown in relationships.

- The philosopher **Immanuel Kant** argued that the basis of ethics is respect for all human beings at all times. Respect is achieved when we always do our duty to each other and expect others to do the same in return. So, if I lie, it would then have to be a duty for me and for all people always to lie. But could we imagine a society in which everyone lied? Would this lead to respect? The answer, according to Kant, is that lying wouldn't create respect as it would cause confusion and mistrust; therefore, it must always be wrong to lie.

- A **utilitarian** might argue that we can only judge whether lying is right or wrong according to the situation, and whether lying would bring about more or less happiness for the greatest number of people.

Each of these ways of thinking assumes that we know what it means to behave ethically, but the reasons for doing so are quite different. This is what makes ethics a philosophically complex and difficult topic.

The basic philosophical problem is that if ethics is about being good, then the question we need to ask is, 'What do you mean by good?'

- For Christians, being good means obeying God's commands.

- For Kantians, it means doing one's duty.

- For utilitarians, such as Mill, it means maximising happiness.

So, who is right? With such different views, this question is by no means easy to answer.

The greatest happiness of the greatest number

John Stuart Mill believed that the basis for ethics was very simple. What all humans desire is to be happy and avoid as much pain as possible. He didn't think he had to prove this as he thought it was obviously what all people want: it makes sense that if I make other people happy, then they will be nicer to me and generally the world will be a more pleasant place to live. So, as Mill says, the utilitarian aim is to create the **greatest happiness of the greatest number**.

Mill shared with his master Jeremy Bentham the view that to some extent it is possible to calculate happiness and pain. This means that in a situation where I am not sure how to act, I can work out what will bring about the greatest amount of happiness for the greatest number. This is particularly helpful in **moral dilemmas** where there could be several different ways in which I could act, but I need a method of deciding rationally whether to do so there is more pleasure and less pain.

▲ I have gone to the cinema with five of my friends and promised to be back home by 9.30 p.m. But my friends want me to go bowling with them for an hour afterwards.

Given the situation in the illustration above, a quick calculation might be:

Pleasure factors	Pain factors
● Being out with my friends	● Feeling guilty for breaking my promise to be home at 9.30 p.m.
● Bowling, which I am good at	● Upsetting my parents
● Not wanting to let my five friends down	● Being punished for being home late
● Showing off my bowling skills	● Being tired the following day and therefore not doing my homework
● Having more down time and therefore being more productive when I do my homework	● Not being considered trustworthy in the future

To make life easier, imagine you attached a numerical value to each of these factors: 10 is a lot of happiness and –10 is a lot of pain. Add them up and then compare. If the totals indicate that going bowling will bring more pleasure than pain, then you should go bowling with your friends. If you calculate that going bowling is going to cause more pain, then you know you ought to return home.

Mill argued that we know from experience that certain actions tend to lead to happiness or unhappiness. For example, we know that being generous to others *tends* to lead to happiness (even though this may not *always* be so). Although we may not make precise calculations as Bentham suggested, we know that there are general moral rules which are taught by society which help guide our decisions. We also know that in some difficult situations these rules are not useful and it is then that we have to abandon the rule and work out the possible consequences ourselves. For this reason, some scholars describe Mill as a **rule utilitarian**.

We can perhaps see now why the utilitarian principle is a powerful method of reforming society and its laws. Many of our laws in the UK have been revised, or abolished, according to the simple and rational utilitarian principle that a good law is one that brings about happiness for society.

Higher and lower pleasures

Mill didn't entirely agree with Bentham about the nature of happiness. He was worried that if ethics is merely about achieving pleasure, then human lives are no different from those of animals. Mill argued that humans are different from animals because we also desire higher pleasures such as listening to music, reading books on philosophy, writing poetry, painting pictures, designing interesting buildings and so on. If we merely aimed to achieve pleasure then society and civilisation would become very boring and unsophisticated. By higher pleasures, Mill meant mental rather than physical activity. So, as he famously said:

> It is better to be a human being dissatisfied than a pig satisfied; **better to be Socrates dissatisfied than a fool satisfied.**

> J.S. Mill, *Utilitarianism*

He meant that he would rather be in a mental state of having to think more about difficult ideas and always be striving to understand (like Socrates) than a person who lives an unsophisticated life by just watching television and going to the pub (like the fool).

However, is it really the case that there are some pleasures that are better than others? Bentham thought not. According to Mill, Bentham claimed that the 'quantity of pleasure being equal, push-pin is as good as poetry'. (The game of push-pin was a popular children's game in eighteenth century.) So, Bentham is claiming that the source of pleasure is largely irrelevant; there are no higher or lower pleasures. If you like playing tennis and I like reading novels and we both gain the same amount of pleasure from them, then tennis is neither superior nor inferior to reading a novel.

But Mill found Bentham's conclusion very unsatisfactory. In his judgement, a civilised society is one that doesn't just aim for basic pleasures but wants humans to develop imaginatively and creatively.

What do you understand? **AO2**

1 Explain what Mill meant when he said, 'It is better to be a human being dissatisfied than a pig satisfied'.

2 Explain what Bentham meant when he said, 'quantity of pleasure being equal, push-pin is as good as poetry'.

What do you think? **AO3**

3 Give three examples of your own higher pleasures and explain why you think they are higher rather than lower pleasures.

Ends and means

It is often said that utilitarians believe 'the ends justify the means': if the 'end' is to maximise happiness, then this justifies the 'means' – the process of doing things to achieve the end, even if these are unpleasant or immoral. Mill was aware that this was a problem.

Activity

In groups, consider whether the following scenarios are justified. Give two reasons for and two reasons against each scenario.

- A criminal has kidnapped a family and is threatening to kill them. The authorities capture and torture the criminal, as the quickest and most efficient means of getting him to tell them where the family is.

- During a war, the commander destroys the enemy stronghold even though he knows that in doing so he will kill some of his own soldiers who are being held captive there.

- You steal food from a supermarket to give to several starving beggars on the street. A lot of the food that has reached its sell-by date will be thrown away at the end of the day anyway.

- You bribe the referee so that the whistle is blown in your favour. You win the match and everyone at school is delighted because your team has beaten the favourites.

Torturing a criminal might bring short-term success.

↓

Others might think that torture is always justified, as it was successful once.

↓

Torture might then become widespread and acceptable.

↓

Perhaps, in the future, a head teacher might use torture to force the truth out of a student, for example, who is suspected of bullying but won't confess to it.

There are many problems when considering whether the ends justify the means. Here are two:

Do we really know the consequences of our actions?

Mill was very aware of this problem. Consequences can have a ripple effect; that is, one result can cause another, which causes another and so on. So, when I calculate a possible 'end' or consequence, how far into the future do I have to look?

Certainly, Mill would regard the use of torture as being generally very bad for society and that even if it could be justified in some extreme cases, there should be a rule which forbids it.

Is there really a distinction between a means and an end?

Essay practice

'Mill's utilitarianism is not a good way to live one's life.' Do you agree? Give reasons for your answer. Show that you have considered more than one point of view.

In the scenario of stealing food from the supermarket to feed the starving beggars, many would argue that what I am doing is not morally good or morally neutral. Stealing is stealing and I am responsible for it. In the chapter on Martin Luther King (see pages 115–122), you will read how King reasoned that disobedience was the 'lesser of two evils'. He fully accepted that what he was doing was not good but believed that obeying an unfair or racist law was worse.

Mill's response to stealing is slightly different. He would not agree with King that stealing is in itself morally wrong. He would probably argue that stealing is wrong only because, in general, it almost always leads to mistrust and worry.

1.4 Martin Luther King's life and thought

Some background to the struggle for civil rights

To understand the struggle for civil rights in the USA, we need to put it in context of the transatlantic slave trade. It is a long and complicated story, but essentially, it begins at the time of Queen Elizabeth I, in the 1500s, when British traders forcibly captured and enslaved people from African countries and then shipped them to America to work on the tobacco **plantations**. This slave trade continued beyond America's independence from Great Britain in 1786. During the nineteenth century, the law was changed, making it illegal to trade in slaves, and in 1865 slavery was abolished.

More and more people realised that slavery was wrong, but the Southern states had made a lot of money from slavery, and from keeping black people as inferior to white people. They got around the law with their own so-called 'Jim Crow' laws (1875), which were based on the principle of 'separate but equal'. This meant separating black people from white people by giving each their own schools, universities, hospitals and even transport. But, the facilities black people were meant to use were often of poorer quality than those used by white people. Although the people were separated from each other, they were not treated equally, as you can see in the photo below. This is the kind of environment Martin Luther King grew up in.

Starter
Is it ever right to disobey the law?

▲ At a bus station in Durham, North Carolina, 1940.

Martin Luther King's life

Martin Luther King (1929–68) was a theologian and Baptist minister. He grew up in Atlanta, Georgia. Shortly after completing his doctorate he found himself leading the black community in their resistance to laws that restricted their human rights and liberties. He was not a theoretical philosopher or theologian because he was primarily concerned with reforming American society. He was assassinated in 1968. The conversation below will help you understand his life and thought.

▲ Martin Luther King junior

Imaginary interview with Dr King

It is 3 April 1968, just as Dr King is finishing giving his speech, 'I've Been to the Mountaintop' to 3000 people at the Mason Temple, Memphis, Tennessee, USA.

King: *(final words of his speech can be heard echoing in the hallway)* '… And I've seen the promised land. I may not get there with you. But I want you to know tonight, that we, as a people will get to the promised land.' *(Dr King emerges from the main hall)*

Journalist: Dr King, Dr King, do you have a moment to answer some questions? I have come all the way from England, but I have been delayed and only managed to hear the end of your speech.

King: Sure. Of course I can. But I have an odd feeling this may be my last speech and probably my last interview. You may think this sounds arrogant, but I see myself like Moses looking into the Promised Land, knowing that justice and liberty is waiting for all my black brothers and sisters – but, like Moses, knowing that I won't be there to see what we have been campaigning for so long to achieve.

Journalist: When did the campaign start? How did you get involved? Why are civil rights such a big issue in the United States?

King: These are all good questions. On 1 December 1955, Mrs Rosa Parks, an activist and seamstress, in Montgomery, Alabama was travelling home on a bus. She chose to sit in a seat marked for white people only. She was told to move, even though the bus was not full. She refused. She was arrested because the laws at the time segregated many areas of life between black people and white people. Her action was the final straw and the black community decided almost overnight to boycott the use of public buses and arrange their own transport. I was a young pastor and had just completed my PhD at Boston University, so the people knew I had the skills to lead and speak on their behalf, and I was duly elected to be the leader of the Montgomery Improvement Association. We decided that the only way to get the authorities to see how unfair, prejudiced and discriminatory the laws of society were, was to disobey them. This has led to my arrest several times and bombs have even been left on the front porch of our home.

Journalist: You mentioned you are a pastor. Could you explain how the Church has played such an important role in your life and your role as a civil rights leader?

King: I was born on 15 January 1929. My mother was called Alberta and my father, the Reverend Martin Luther King senior, was the minister of Ebenezer Baptist Church. So, you can see that Christianity and Christian ministry was in my blood. But there is more to it than this. The black churches don't just meet on a Sunday, they support many local activities and are a natural meeting point for the black community. The black churches have a strong sense of Jesus as the one who suffers with them and that gives them courage to carry on.

Journalist: So, have all the black churches fully supported the rights movement?

King: No, you are right in what you are suggesting. My early policy was for non-violent direct action. In 1957 Corretta, my wife, and I travelled to India as guests of the Indian Prime Minister Jawaharlal Nehru so we could study the techniques and effects of one my great heroes, Mahatma Gandhi. He showed how by disobeying the laws peacefully you could bring about great changes to society. But not all my black pastor friends agree. They think we should be patient and wait for God to bring about change at the right time. In 1963 when I was in Birmingham, Alabama, helping them protest against segregation, I was arrested and imprisoned. This gave me the opportunity to write the *Letter from Birmingham Jail* to black and white pastors to explain why, even as Christians, in extreme circumstances the law has to be broken.

Journalist: So, have you been successful in your non-violent protests?

King: In some ways, sadly not. Many have suffered brutal treatment – far-right white groups have murdered black activists and the authorities have turned a blind eye, the police themselves have beaten us ordinary black people and used pressurised water hoses against demonstrators. And yet, to quote our slogan, 'we shall overcome'. Everyone knows of the crowning moment on 28 August 1963 when a crowd of some 250,000 gathered in Washington DC. I joined many other leaders and, on the steps of the Lincoln Memorial, delivered my speech 'I Have a Dream'. I suppose, after that,

the most significant event was when the Voting Rights Act finally became law in 1965. At last, black Americans were given the same voting rights as white Americans.

Journalist: You must have thought that this marked the end of your campaigning.

King: Far from it. It was just the beginning. We still have to change hearts and minds, and besides there are many other social problems to fight against – associated with rights for black as well as white people – housing, healthcare and continued problems of race violence. We now have to get more black people elected into local government, to help make sure that the law is applied and that black people are recognised as being fully part of society. I have also campaigned against the Vietnam War, for which I was greatly honoured by being awarded the Nobel Peace Prize in 1964. Not everyone approves – I am considered unpatriotic and in Chicago an angry white crowd threw stones at me because I had campaigned for housing to be available to blacks and whites equally in the city.

Journalist: Dr King, you have given generously of your time, and I can see you want to be getting back to your hotel after an exhausting day.

King: Thank you for your questions, and remember, 'we shall overcome'.

The following day (4 April 1968), as Martin Luther King stood on the balcony of the Lorraine Motel, Memphis, he was shot by James Earl Ray. Shortly afterwards he died in hospital.

What do you know? AO1

1 Outline the main events of Martin Luther King's life.
2 Outline the historical reasons which had led to black/white segregation in the USA.

What do you understand? AO2

3 Explain the significance of Christianity in King's life.
4 Why was King often regarded as a troublemaker and unpatriotic?
5 Explain the importance of Mahatma Gandhi on King's thought.

Martin Luther King's teaching

The dream of equality

Martin Luther King had a dream, a dream which was both political and theological. In some ways, he shared Plato's vision that society could be transformed by working towards the ideal. But whereas for Plato the 'Good' is an abstract, otherworldly ideal, for King the ideal is personal and worldly. As a Christian thinker, his inspiration was the Bible's depiction of God's kingdom on Earth, in events such as Moses' quest for the promised land, in Jesus' teaching on the Kingdom of God and the image of the 'New Jerusalem' as used by the author of the Book of Revelation to describe the world transformed into a place of peace, love and justice.

Although King's ideas were firmly rooted in philosophical and theological arguments, his means of conveying his ideas were not through dialogues or books but mainly by giving speeches and sermons. For him, the test of a successful argument was whether it could bring about *actual* change.

▲ Martin Luther King gives his famous speech at the Lincoln Memorial, 28 August 1963.

For example, probably his most famous speech was the one he delivered at the Lincoln Memorial in Washington, DC in 1963, known as the 'I Have a Dream' speech (although he had already given similar versions of the speech as sermons). The speech ends famously with his vision of a society where black people and white people of different Christian traditions will join hands and sing the words of the old Negro spiritual, 'Free at last. Free at last. Thank God Almighty, we are free at last.'

The speech relies heavily on the use of metaphors and imagery to stir up the crowd and help them to understand the ideas of the civil rights protest movement. The speech mixes theological ideas with the political ideals on which the United States was founded, the so-called **American dream** of life, liberty and happiness for all. One of the metaphors King uses describes how the American dream has become a lie, an 'I owe you' note or a cheque which the issuer has no intention of honouring, even though they may have the means of paying. But, says King, a promise is a promise, and that is why the promise of the American Constitution that 'all men are created equal' has now to be demanded.

King compares himself to the Old Testament prophets such as Isaiah, who preached freedom and justice not just for oppressed people of Israel but for all. Towards the end of his speech, King quotes the image of justice and equality which the prophet Isaiah uses. Isaiah describes a time when all the valleys in the world are filled in and mountains flattened so that the world is a level playing field and all people are treated equally in God's world.

Every valley shall be raised up,
every mountain and hill made low;
... And the glory of the Lord will be revealed,
and all mankind together will see it.

Isaiah 40:4–5

Justice and fairness

King's *Letter from Birmingham Jail* (16 April 1963) sets out clearly his theological and philosophical ideas of justice and justification for civil disobedience. King responds to the criticism from many black and white clergy that his actions were untimely and would do more harm than good. King's answer is that there is no such thing as a good or bad time when it comes to implementing justice. He argues that justice is universal and that at the time he is writing people in many different parts of world people are seeking radical changes which will end racial injustice. Laws which prohibit justice, he says, must be met with protest, because, 'an unjust law is no law at all' and 'injustice anywhere is a threat to justice everywhere'.

His notion of universal justice is based on the theological premise that if all human beings are created in the **image of God**, then it follows that each and every person is entitled to the same rights and equality of treatment whatever their colour, race and class. Justice means treating each person with respect as a person and not as a thing as if they don't exist. An unjust law is one which the majority or those with power compel the minority to keep to but do not apply to themselves. King's example of gross injustice is the fact that the majority of white adult people were allowed to vote but denied the vote to black adults.

> **Activity**
> Make a poster by copying out one of quotations above from the 'I Have a Dream' speech and illustrating it with your drawings, and key ideas and photos from Martin Luther King's life.

Civil disobedience and non-violent direct action

Justice too long delayed is justice denied.

Martin Luther King, *Letter from Birmingham Jail*

The catchphrase of the civil rights movement was 'we shall overcome'. King considered it to refer to both sides of the same coin: theologically it referred to the biblical hope of God's justice flowing down to wipe out injustice, hatred and poverty; politically it got the Churches to move into the streets and to challenge the law. But his opponents (black and white) criticised him for being undemocratic; they argued that it is never right to break the law. King's *Letter from Birmingham Jail* argues that it is right to break a human law when:

● a law fails to conform to God's eternal and natural law

● a law fails to uphold human dignity or personality

● a law breaker accepts the consequences of breaking the law (e.g. imprisonment)

● a law breaker does so lovingly, openly and in good conscience.

A person who breaks the law, therefore, is in fact showing a great deal of respect for the law, as their actions are there to improve society and enable justice for all. King's critics accused him of breaking Jesus' teaching that a Christian has a duty to obey the authorities. Jesus commanded, 'Give back what is due to Caesar what is Caesar's and to God what is God's' (Mark 12.17). But King gives the example from the Book of Daniel, in the Old Testament, where Shadrach, Meshach and Abednego refused to obey King Nebuchadnezzar's laws because these conflicted with God's higher laws (Daniel 3).

Another issue King addressed in his *Letter from Birmingham Jail* is the accusation from other Christian leaders that his civil rights movement has led to unchristian and unlawful behaviour such as demonstrations which have caused violence, bombings and deaths. King's reply was that in a situation of gross injustice where local leaders fail to negotiate, non-violent direct action (such as **sit-ins**, marches, disobedience, **boycotts**) are the only alternative.

The aim of the protests was indeed to cause disruption and 'tensions in the community' (just as Socrates did through his method of teaching the young men of Athens to think for themselves and challenge the law) but avoid direct violence.

▲ Martin Luther King in Birmingham jail.

The justification of the use of force in Christianity has always been problematic. Some philosophers have argued that non-violence has the same moral status of violence, if it leads to injustice and suffering. Controlled violence such as that used in war, can lead to less suffering and greater good. But King was not persuaded. He called his position **realistic pacifism**, which accepts that although non-violent direct action may indirectly cause suffering, it is nevertheless justified (because it is the lesser of two evils) whereas direct violence is always evil. The realistic pacifist accepts that if their actions cause harm then they are not sinless and they must accept any blame which follows – but to fail to act at all would be a cause of a greater evil.

Finally, King argued that the ends do *not* justify the means; non-violent means must be good in themselves, even if good ends are not achieved. Far worse, King argues, are those who use moral means (such as maintaining law and order) to preserve an unjust society.

What do you understand? AO2

1 Explain three reasons why it is always wrong to break the law.

2 Explain what King meant when he said, 'an unjust law is no law at all'.

3 Explain why King argued that it is sometimes right to disobey the law.

4 Explain what King meant by 'realistic pacifism'.

What do you think? AO3

5 Supposing the headteacher made it a rule that all children with blue eyes must clean the toilets every day. Any child who refused would be severely punished and extra chores would be imposed on the other blue-eyed children. Which of the following would you do? Give reasons for your answers.

   a Carry out the rule and then arrange to meet the headteacher and persuade her to change the rule.

   b Refuse to carry out the rule.

   c Kidnap the headteacher and refuse to release her until she abolishes the rule.

   d Destroy the toilets.

The beloved community

King calls his vision of reformed America 'the beloved community'. It is a community based on mutual respect, love and justice. But is it really a possibility? Doesn't selfish human nature make this impossible?

In his sermon 'Unfulfilled Dreams' (1968), King argued that our good intentions are often destroyed by selfishness. In the New Testament, St Paul summarises this sinful aspect of human nature as follows:

> *For I have the desire to do what is good, but I cannot carry it out. For I do not do the good I want to do, but the evil I do not want to do – this I keep on doing. Now if I do what I do not want to do, it is no longer I who do it, but it is sin living in me that does it.*

Romans 7.18–20

The solution is that through faith and belief in the transforming love of God, whenever humans intend good, however incomplete, God's grace makes it a possibility. Only in this way will the dream of justice and freedom ever have any chance of succeeding. Suffering therefore has a purpose. Black people have suffered for centuries in the USA, but it has given them the strength and courage to protest so that others might go free. King was inspired by Isaiah's example of the suffering servant (Isaiah 53) and Jesus' life, death and resurrection. Both the suffering servant and Jesus suffered and died to stir up the consciences of others to establish a better society.

What do you think? **AO3**

1 Is there any point in striving for a better society if humans are essentially selfish?
2 Does suffering make us better people?
3 Is society progressing for the better?

Essay practice

'If everyone was allowed to pick and choose which laws they wanted to obey, chaos would follow.' Do you agree? Give reasons for your answer. Show that you have considered more than one point of view.

What are ethics?

Everyday debates

In the media, at home, at school and among our friends we constantly discuss what is the right way and wrong way of behaving: what are good and bad actions. Look at these three newspaper articles as examples of everyday discussions about what is or is not morally acceptable.

Punish parents who let underage children play video games

A report released recently by a children's charity said that parents should be fined or given prison sentences if it were found they were allowing their children to play video games when they were underage. Pauline Winter for the charity said, 'The reason why video games are given an age rating is to stop children from being mentally harmed by viewing unsuitable material. We should make an example of parents who behave irresponsibly.'

The report was immediately condemned by Richard Fall of the parents' group Parental Liberty. 'This is just another example of the nanny state trying to interfere with our freedom. Surely, we as parents know what is best for our children. Some children are more mature than others so we should decide …'

Sprinter Smith found guilty of taking performance drugs

Yesterday, the sprinter John Smith was found guilty of taking drugs which the sports council said helped build up his muscles giving him an unfair advantage over other athletes.

Smith was unrepentant and said in court, 'There are lots of things an athlete can use to give himself an advantage on the track. He might wear the latest running shoes, he might train more than his rivals, he might attend yoga classes to help his concentration. Taking these drugs was just another means of achieving my goal. I don't think what I did was wrong.'

A council member said, 'Taking performance drugs is always wrong as it undermines the competition which tests all the athletes' skill at running …'

Hero or villain?

On the third day of his trial, Captain Nick Worthington was cross-questioned by the prosecution as to his actions in Iraq in what has become the notorious 'Red Thunder' case. Captain Worthington is accused of torturing three Iraqi soldiers to gain information to save the lives of ten captured British soldiers.

Torture of any kind is strictly forbidden in the United Nation's Universal Declaration of Human Rights, article 5. The prosecution accused Captain Worthington of acting cruelly by depriving the Iraqi soldiers of light and food until they said where the soldiers were being held hostage.

Captain Worthington denied that he had used cruel, inhuman or degrading treatment. 'In war,' he said, 'we have to act very fast otherwise many lives might be lost. We knew that we didn't have long before our men were to be executed by the enemy. Depriving our captives of light and food for several days was justified …'

Moral values

Acceptable behaviour is called **morality**. Morality is based on **ethical principles**; these principles guide us as to what is right and wrong. However, there is no agreement on how these ethical principles are formed and which ones are ultimately right. You have probably learnt certain ethical principles from your parents and from your teachers. Some of these principles might be based on what is socially acceptable behaviour, some might be taught through a religion, other principles might be based on common sense or conscience.

Knowing exactly what ethics are is complex. As we saw in the chapter 'What is philosophy?' (pages 93–97), the role of philosophy in situations such as this is to ask basic questions.

One of these questions might be: what do we think we mean when we say something is right or fair or just? Philosophy aims to make clear or **clarify** what ethics are and why it is that we often strongly disagree about our **moral values**.

Duties and consequences

When philosophers analyse people's moral values, they notice that ethical principles tend to fall into two kinds: those that are based on duties and those that focus mostly on consequences.

Duty ethics

Duty ethicists believe that living a good life means being obedient to a rule or duty. For example, in the Bible the **Ten Commandments** (Exodus 20.1–17) set out some important rules which are required if we are to live civilised lives. What would society be like if there were no rule not to steal, or if adultery were just a matter of opinion, or if murder were acceptable, or if lying were normal? Duty ethicists consider being obedient and carrying out moral duties requires effort, determination and discipline; these are qualities that make us moral people.

Consequential ethics

Consequential ethicists believe that although rules might be helpful, living a good life usually means working out what will make us happy or content. This means judging what will have good or bad consequences. Sometimes lying can have good consequences and sometimes it causes harm. For the consequentialist, always doing one's duty and being obedient to the rules means that you regard the rules as being more important than people; that is not behaving ethically.

What do you understand? (AO2)

4 Explain what duty ethicists believe.

5 Explain what consequentialist ethicists believe.

What do you know? (AO1)

1 What is morality?

2 What are ethical principles?

3 What are the Ten Commandments?

Essay practice

'There is nothing wrong with breaking a promise if the consequences are good.' Do you agree? Give reasons for your answer. Show that you have considered more than one point of view.

Moral dilemmas

A moral dilemma is caused when two or more duties clash or when a good action might also lead to a bad consequence. How do we decide what to do?

This is when philosophers look very carefully at different ethical theories to see how the dilemmas have been caused and how they might be solved. The chapters that follow will raise many examples of moral dilemmas.

What do you think? (AO3)

6 Look up the Prisoner's Dilemma. What does this tell you about some of the problems of consequential ethics?

Topic 2 Ethics

2.1 Life and death

Is life valuable?

What makes human life valuable and worth living? The answer isn't immediately obvious. Throughout human history, and in various parts of the world today, many human lives are not considered valuable. There are many examples of humans being used as cheap labour and as slaves by other humans.

Starter

Is killing always wrong?

Human trafficking still takes place in many parts of the world today, and in many societies children and women are still considered to be inferior to men.

In the nineteenth century social reformers and philosophers such as John Stuart Mill worked from a very simple observation that as all humans are rational and capable of feeling happiness and pain, then everyone should be treated equally. It is for these reasons that Mill campaigned for women to have equal rights with men. See pages 109–114 for more about John Stuart Mill's argument for women's rights.

▲ Why is it that some people are treated as only having monetary value?

The quality of life principle

The word used to describe the capacity to reason and feel pain and pleasure is **sentience**. There is considerable debate as to when the human foetus becomes sentient, and whether all non-human animals experience sentience. Sentience is very important in making moral decisions. For example, someone who is severely brain damaged may be said to have very little sentience and therefore the quality of their life might be so poor that death might be considered the better option. This argument is based on the **quality of life principle**.

Issues such as abortion, euthanasia, the death penalty and war are controversial moral issues because the loss of a human life is the loss of something very special and valuable, but there may be times when the loss of a life is necessary.

Sanctity of life principle

The sanctity of life principle is usually a religious idea about human life. In Christian theology, a person's life is valuable not merely because the person is sentient, but because he or she is created in the **image of God**. Being made in the image of God means that every person has a soul or unique personality. In other words, all human life is equally valuable because it is a **God-given** gift which only God can take away. The sanctity of life principle means that from the moment of **conception**, when a person's life begins, that person's life is sacred and must be protected. Any ending of a life, such as by abortion or euthanasia, is morally unacceptable.

Activity

Charlie Gard suffered from a rare genetic disorder. Great Ormond Street Hospital doctors calculated that taking him to the USA for experimental treatment, as his parents wanted, would not be in the child's best interests and he should be allowed to die.

Read the information about Charlie Gard. In groups, discuss the two viewpoints below. Set out the strengths and weaknesses of each view.

- From a non-religious and utilitarian point of view, the doctors' decision was right as the quality of Charlie's life was so low that prolonging his life would be cruel and would not lead to a happy life.

- From a Christian point of view, Charlie is a person made in the image of God and loved and wanted by his parents. The doctors' decision was wrong. Charlie should not be allowed to die but should be given every opportunity to live.

What do you know? AO1

1 What does the word 'sentience' mean?

2 What does the phrase 'image of God' mean for Christians?

3 What does it mean to say that life begins at conception?

What do you understand? AO2

4 Explain why some people are treated as being less valuable than others.

5 Explain what is meant by the quality of life principle.

6 Explain what is meant by the sanctity of life principle.

Life after death

The question of what makes life worth living also depends on whether you think this life is:

- preparation for a life after death, or

- all that there is, and when we die, that is the end (there is no life after death).

Both views influence the way we behave and what aspects of life we value.

Nihilism

The word 'nihilism' comes from the Latin word meaning 'nothing'. There are many different forms of nihilism, from the optimistic to the pessimistic.

The most extreme form of nihilism says that there is nothing we can know for certain – we can't even know whether what we experience is real or not. Nihilists don't believe God exists and they reject that there is life after death, because when we die our bodies decompose and that is the end of our existence.

The pessimistic nihilist sees little point in life; it is just something to be endured. Ernest Hemingway (1899–1961), the famous novelist, took this view. He compares life to walking in a dark passage leading nowhere.

> *For him it was a dark passage which led to nowhere, then to nowhere, then again to nowhere, once again to nowhere.*
>
> Ernest Hemingway, *For Whom the Bell Tolls*

Albert Camus (1913–60), the French philosopher and novelist, also explored the idea of nihilism in his novel *The Outsider*. The novel begins with the chief character, Meursault, unsure whether his mother has died today or yesterday. It appears that nihilism is a pessimistic view of life. Meursault leads a meaningless life, for as he says at one point, 'I'd lived in a certain way and could just as well have lived in a different way. I'd done one thing whereas I had not done another. So what?'

▲ Albert Camus

Then Meursault accidenty shoots a person and is imprisoned, but he doesn't appear to care whether he will be executed. Then he has a moment of sudden self-awareness. He sees that being a nihilist doesn't mean being indifferent to the world and living life as if in a dream, but being alive to its endless possibilities. He has become an optimistic nihilist.

The optimistic nihilist believes that, as we only get one chance at life, then it is up to us to be as creative, imaginative and inventive as possible. As there is no God to judge us, and no fear of hell or heaven after death, then we are free to choose whatever we think will lead to a fulfilling life.

But optimistic nihilism requires a lot of effort. As the philosopher Jean-Paul Sartre argues, a lot of people are lazy and hide from the view that life is essentially meaningless by lying to themselves and pretending to be people they are not. Others escape by having lavish lifestyles or taking drugs. Escapism is not real life. Real life is one of commitment: commitment in one's relationships, to one's job, to one's political beliefs and so on.

Resurrection

Christianity, Islam and Judaism all teach that after death a person's soul and body is resurrected and lives on. This presents many difficult philosophical problems as to what kind of existence this might be, but the importance of resurrection is what it implies for human life in this world. You can read about Muslim and Jewish beliefs about resurrection and life after death in the other book in this series, *Religion for Common Entrance 13+*.

The starting point in Christianity is the experience that the disciples had of Jesus' resurrection after his death. According to the New Testament, many people saw the risen Jesus for a long time after his death, for example, in the Gospel of John 20.24–29. Some interpret these encounters as powerful visions of Jesus, some as actual meetings with him, but whatever happened these experiences confirmed in the minds of those who experienced them, that death was not the end of life.

St Paul argued that Jesus' resurrection made it possible for everyone to be raised after death to eternal life, as it is often referred to in the New Testament.

The philosophical questions about what is actually meant by resurrection are extremely difficult to answer. Here are various Christian suggestions:

What do you know? **AO1**

1 Name two kinds of nihilists.

2 What does the word 'resurrection' mean?

- At the last judgement each person's soul will be reunited with its earthly body. The unrighteous will live eternally in hell and the righteous in heaven.

- At the last judgement each person's soul will be reunited with its body, but this body will not be a physical body but a spiritual version of it. The unrighteous resurrected person will live eternally in hell and the righteous in heaven.

- At death the body decays but the person's soul lives on and is judged by God as to whether it can enter heaven or hell.

- At death a person's soul continues its journey. Hell is not a place but the experience the soul has of not being united with God. All souls have the potential of being united with God in the heavenly state.

What do you understand? **AO2**

3 Why do Christians believe in life after death?

4 Explain what is meant by heaven and hell.

5 Explain how a belief in resurrection might affect a person's attitude to others.

So how might the idea of resurrection affect a person's moral values? The thought that one will be judged by God and rewarded with heaven or hell might encourage one to live morally, according to God's laws as enshrined in the Bible and Church teaching. Resurrection might indicate that all humans have souls which make them more than just animals, and so deserving of respect (however despicable their lifestyle might be). Resurrection reinforces the sanctity of life principle.

What do you think? **AO3**

6 Discuss which of the four explanations above (the bullet points) you think makes the most sense.

Reincarnation

Reincarnation is different from resurrection. Reincarnation means that the self or soul does not continue on after death in the same body (whether this is a physical or spiritual body), but enters into a new body in this world.

The Hindu view of reincarnation

- Every living thing is essentially spirit, or atman. When the atman lives in a particular body it is called jivatman.

- All physical things change. Living things are born; they grow, develop, decay and then die, but they reproduce and new life follows. The seasons follow on from each other in a cycle of change. This cycle of birth–death–birth is called samsara or reincarnation.

- You have already been through some cycles of samsara; first you began as a fertilised egg, then a foetus, then a baby, then a toddler, then a child, then soon to be an adult. Although you have been through many physical changes, your essential self or atman (jivatman) has remained the same. The aim though is to be released from the cycle or rebirths and to achieve enlightenment or moksha. In this state, atman becomes blissfully reunited with Brahman who is the spiritual source of everything.

- Samsara is governed by the law of cause and effect (or karma). Generally, if you are a good person, you will be reborn into a good life, in the next cycle. This is easy to observe in the human world where some people are naturally more spiritual and morally advanced than others. This suggests that in their former lives they had done fewer bad things, which had negative karmic results.

- So how might the idea of reincarnation affect a person's moral values? It might make them value all living beings, as they all possess atman and are connected to all of us at a spiritual level. If we mistreat other human beings and non-human beings, then this will have negative karmic effects on them and on our future existence. Reincarnation reinforces the sanctity of life principle. If we desire enlightenment and a future blissful existence, then we know we have many lifetimes to work to achieve moral perfection.

Objections

- There are many philosophical objections to reincarnation, mainly that despite claims of remembering former lives (often done under hypnosis), there is no evidence that this is an actual memory of the atman.

- A moral objection is that a belief in reincarnation makes a person morally lazy because they might think they can spend many lifetimes behaving better, rather than aiming for perfection now.

What do you think? **AO3**

5 Does belief in reincarnation make us more or less respectful of life?

What do you understand? **AO2**

1 Explain how reincarnation is different from resurrection.

2 Why do Hindus believe in reincarnation?

3 Explain the relationship between atman and samsara.

4 What is the relationship between samsara and karma?

Ethics of war and pacifism

Why war?

We need to have the option of war to protect our way of life against our enemies.

War is necessary to expand our territory and increase our country's wealth.

▲ A Syrian national army tank close to a war zone in the city of Damascus, Syria, September 2013.

If someone attacks us then we should fight back.

War expresses strength and commitment to our national values.

War is a last resort to protect the innocent.

Some people argue that war is just a fact of life. There are aggressive and dangerous leaders in the world, and if we didn't oppose them then we would be allowing evil to rule in the world. This is called the war realist's view.

Others argue that wars can bring a nation together. During war, national values are much clearer and we show other nations what we really believe in. This is called the war militarist view. Holy wars (wars fought for religious reasons, such as the Crusades) and political wars (such Russia's invasion of Ukraine) are examples of **war militarism**.

Just war

Although the just war argument has its origins in Christianity, today many people support it whether they have religious views or not. Just war is a war realist view that wars are sometimes necessary but they are never good. War is considered to be the lesser of two evils, and a last resort where the ends justify the means. The 'just' in just war, therefore, means justified, fair and legal.

There are three parts to the modern just war arguments: justification for going to war; justice in war; justice after war.

Justification for going to war

- There must be a **just cause** such as defence of the land or protection of innocent people.
- The war must be **authorised** by a democratic government.
- The **intentions** and motives must be good; war must be to resist evil and promote good.
- It must have a reasonable **chance of success**.
- It must be the **last resort**. All other possibilities must be explored first.
- The use of war must be **proportionate** to the result it wishes to achieve.

Justice in war

- The means used in the battle field must be **proportionate**; force must be kept to the minimum.
- Those who are **non-combatants** (all those on either side who are not soldiers) must be **protected**.

Justice after war

- The victors must **restore** law and order.
- The environment must be **protected** (i.e. further destruction must not take place) and made habitable.

Activity

Find out about a particular war (it may be one you have been studying in history). More recent wars include: the First Gulf War (1990–91), the Iraq War and the Second Gulf War (2003–11).

Apply the just war principles to it and consider whether it was a 'just war'. Scholars are divided as to whether *all* the conditions have to be fulfilled or just the majority. Discuss this in class or in your group. Finally, you could present your findings as the front page of a newspaper. The headline might be 'First Gulf War – not just!' or 'Was the Falklands War just?'

Pacifism

All pacifists believe that if it is morally wrong for individuals to kill another human being, then it is even worse for there to be mass killing in war. Pacifists might base their views on the sanctity of life principle or the quality of life principle. Because different people have different reasons for their pacifist beliefs, there are different versions of pacifism.

In philosophy the word 'weak' is sometimes used to mean that a principle may have exceptions. For example, if I am a weak rule moralist, then it means that sometimes a rule may be broken for good reasons.

Here are two versions of pacifism: absolute pacifism and weak pacifism.

> **Absolute pacifists** believe that as there is, based on the sanctity of life principle, never any justification for the use of violence then all war is morally wrong. Christian absolute pacifists quote Jesus' teaching that we should love our enemies and forgive those who hate us. He also taught that it is the peacemakers who will be blessed and he told Peter to put away his sword when he was being arrested at Gethsemane.
>
> As an absolute pacifist Martin Luther King insisted that the best means of bringing about change and resisting evil was through non-violent direct action such as refusing to carry out bad laws, striking, marches, trade sanctions and so on. (See pages 120–121 for more on Martin Luther King's use of non-violent direct action.)

> **Weak pacifists** believe that violence and war should only be used as the **very last resort** when all other options have failed. Many weak pacifists base their argument on the utilitarian quality of life principle that it is sometimes better, for long-term peace and happiness, to fight a war. Based on the utilitarian principle that the ends justify the means, killing in war, though not desirable, is inevitable and justified. For these reasons, many weak pacifists support the just war argument but only when the aim of a just war is peace and the use of force is minimal.

Christians are divided about whether they should support absolute or weak pacifism. Jesus' teaching is ambiguous. Some argue that Jesus' teaching in the Sermon on the Mount to love one's enemies only sets up an ideal of pacifism but that in an imperfect and sinful world, war may have to be used. Furthermore Jesus did not condemn soldiers and he did not say anything explicitly against war. Finally, Jesus also taught that Christians should obey the state, so if the state orders that its citizens should fight, then Christians must obey.

On the other hand, in the Sermon on the Mount, Jesus said the use of violence (an eye for an eye) should be replaced by reconciliation. He also taught that as the Kingdom of God is how the world should be then Christians have a duty to carry out its ideals now and create a world of peace. This can only be done by being an absolute pacifist.

Essay practice

'War is never right. There are always better ways of resolving conflict.' Do you agree? Give reasons for your answer. Show that you have considered more than one point of view.

What do you know? AO1

1 Give two reasons for going to war.
2 What is a just war?
3 What is justice after war?

What do you understand? AO2

3 Explain what it means to use proportionate means in war.
4 Explain what absolute pacifists believe.
5 Explain what weak pacifists believe.

2.2 Punishment

Why punish?

Starter

What is punishment for?

Activity

Read the two scenarios below.

1 Plagiarism

Simon has got very behind with his homework. He is not good at English and he has to produce a 200-word essay on the Shakespeare play they are studying by Friday. He knows that Clare has written her essay and has left it in her school locker. So, at lunchtime, he borrows Clare's essay and copies it out, putting in a few ideas of his own. Not surprisingly, the following week, Simon is summoned by his English teacher and accused of **plagiarism** (copying someone's work without their permission and passing it off as one's own).

2 Snapchat scandal

Mike is captain of the first team at football and everyone likes him. Sarah wants Mike to notice her, but he hasn't paid her much attention. Sarah is annoyed with Mike for ignoring her, so she decides to create a photo of him kissing a Year 7 girl and to send it via Snapchat to everyone in Year 8. The effect is stunning! Soon everyone is talking about Mike but now he's not quite the hero he was. Some people think he has behaved very badly.

In groups, consider the following:

a Why should Simon and Sarah be punished?

b Explain what punishment you would give to Simon.

c Explain what punishment you would give to Sarah.

d Imagine you are the headteacher. You are meeting the parents of Simon and Sarah to explain the reasons why their children are being punished. Role-play the conversations. What would you say to the parents? What do you think the parents would say?

The feeling that someone ought to be punished for wrongdoing is a very basic human response. If someone wrongs you, the desire to 'get your own back' is quite natural. We call this **revenge**. How often have you experienced the tit-for-tat feeling – my sister messes up my room, so I'll go and mess up her room? However, punishment is not the same as revenge, for the following reasons:

- In the examples of Simon and Sarah, punishment is decided and delivered by an authority (the head teacher who represents the school).

- There has to be a general recognition that the authority is allowed to do this (the children's parents agree to the head teacher's decision).

- There has to be a sense that the punishment is fair and morally acceptable and fair (everyone knows the school rules).

▲ What is the difference between revenge and punishment?

Revenge is different. Revenge does not require an authority to decide whether harming the culprit is reasonable or morally acceptable or fair.

However, the distinction between revenge and punishment is very fine. The moral reasons for both revenge and punishment are often hard to justify. Philosophers have debated for thousands of years why, generally, when somebody does something bad, society then inflicts something bad on to them. It does seem that two wrongs are thought to make a right.

But even though the feeling of outrage, and desire to right a wrong, are important aspects of punishment, it serves other social purposes as well. When you discussed the Simon and Sarah cases, you probably recognised that punishment is also aimed at those who have *not* yet committed an offence, and also to reassure others, who do keep to the rules, that offenders don't gain unfairly by breaking the rules.

Some important words:

Offender: a person who has committed a crime by breaking the law

Juvenile offenders: young offenders aged ten to eighteen

Reoffender: someone who has offended, been in prison, and then commits another crime or offence

Inmate: an offender who is being held in prison

Victim: a person who has a crime or offence committed against them

Revenge: harm done to someone in retaliation for harm they have done to someone else

Just deserts: an appropriate punishment for a crime or offence

Rehabilitation: the process of helping an offender to adjust back into society

Custody: being held in prison or an equivalent place of detainment

Aims of punishment

There are four general aims of punishment: retribution, deterrence, protection and reform. All four aims overlap with each other.

Retribution. Retribution is very close to the experience of revenge. Retribution pays back the offender for the harm they have caused to others. It is the most ancient guiding principle of punishment and is often referred to by the Latin phrase *lex talionis* or the 'law of the retaliation'.

It can be found in the Old Testament laws on punishment, summarised by the phrase 'an eye for an eye, a tooth for a tooth'. In other words, the offender receives their 'just deserts' for the crime they have committed by being made to experience the same harm.

Another aspect to retribution is that of 'fair play'. If I keep within the speed limit on the motorway and you break it, it is only fair that you should not be allowed to drive (for a while) as punishment. In other words, those who respect the law should be rewarded by the equivalent rights of those who break it being taken away.

Deterrence. If rules and laws are there to maximise people's happiness and freedoms, then those who break the rules should be punished, to deter or put off others who think they can also break the rules. Punishment is to warn those who think they can 'get away with it' that this is not the case. Examples of deterrence include: fines, community service, imprisonment and the death penalty.

Deterrence is also designed to stop the offender from reoffending and committing further crimes.

Protection. This aim of punishment is very different from the first two. Its purpose is not to inflict pain on the offender but to protect society from further harm caused by the offender. It is also to protect offenders from causing more harm to themselves by carrying out more crimes and making themselves more socially unacceptable.

Reform. This follows on from punishment as protection, but it goes further. Reform punishment aims to make offenders see the error of their ways, and to change and ultimately to be **rehabilitated** into society. For example, offenders might learn new skills in prison or acquire qualifications which will help them find work in society when they are released from prison.

What do you know? {AO1}

1 What is the *lex talionis*?

2 What is the difference between an offender and a reoffender?

3 What is rehabilitation?

What do you understand? {AO2}

4 Explain the aims of punishment as deterrence and as reform.

5 Explain how revenge is different from punishment.

Prison

▲ This prison has been designed based on Jeremy Bentham's 'panopticon' prison – so that the inmates have the impression that they are being observed all the time. This is meant to help them change their behaviour. The aim of the design, Bentham said, was to be 'a mill for grinding rogues honest'. How do you think the panopticon helps offenders to reform?

Prison is one of the most common means of punishing offenders today. Over the past century, prisons have undergone major changes as society has reformed its views about the aims of punishment. In the past, prison or jail (or gaol) was used to remove criminals from the street or to hold one's enemies as prisoners. Conditions were often very poor and there was no sense that the offender might reform. All this changed in the late nineteenth century. Christian social reformers were motivated by Christian teaching on repentance – that sinners or offenders should be given the opportunity to see the errors of their ways and change. Utilitarian reformers, such as Jeremy Bentham and John Stuart Mill, argued that prisons should not be there purely to inflict pain, but to treat offenders humanely in the hope that they would change their ways and learn how to become useful members of society.

Ethical issues of prison

Prison has to fulfil all the various aims of punishment depending on the crime committed. The ethical challenge is how to get the right balance between the retribution and reform.

Many people feel that often prison is too soft on inmates and that they should not have access to television, computers and other luxuries. The point of prison, as they see it, is to be retributive and a deterrent. They believe that this won't happen if life in prison is too pleasant and that prison is meant to be tough.

Others argue that prison will always be tough because, unlike life for ordinary citizens, life in prison removes one of things we value most: freedom. The prison routine means you have to get up at a certain time, have your meals at set times, and return to your room or cell when told to do so. Loss of freedom is the single biggest retributive aspect of prison. Even when someone has been released from prison and is on **parole**, their freedom is restricted so they are still being punished. Therefore, although prison may appear to be a soft punishment, lack of freedom means in reality that it is a far from pleasant experience.

Prison reform

Despite the improvements made to the prison system, many people consider that prison is not effective in its aims as a place of protection, deterrence and reform.

Organisations such as the **Prison Reform Trust** campaign to make prison the place of last resort for serious and violent offenders, and to use alternative punishments for offenders such as fines, community service, electronic tagging and suspended sentences.

Aim of punishment	Why prison is not effective
Protection	• Prisons don't protect inmates from the bad influences of other inmates. • Some argue that prisons can be 'universities of crime' where offenders learn more about criminal activity rather than change their ways.
Deterrence	• According to UK government statistics for 2014–15 the proven rate of adults reoffending after being released from prison was 23.8% and 37.8% for juvenile offenders. These are just proven cases, so the reality is that the numbers of inmates reoffending is probably much higher. • Critics of the prison system argue that this shows that for almost a quarter of all inmates prison is not effective in reducing crime.
Reform	• In 2015–16, there were approximately 85,500 prison inmates in England and Wales, 7,700 in Scotland and 1,600 in Northern Ireland. That is equivalent to 0.13% of the population. • The rate is increasing every year, making the UK prison population one of the highest in the western world. The prison population of England and Wales rose by about 90% between 1990 and 2016. • Prisons depersonalise offenders rather than helping them reform. • Overcrowding leads to a lack of resources (such as education, occupational therapy, new skills) and the inability to help inmates adjust to the outside world.

What do you know? AO1

1 Outline the Christian reasons for prison.
2 Outline the utilitarian reasons for prison.
3 Name two different kinds of prisons.

What do you understand? AO2

4 Explain why some argue that modern prisons are too soft on prisoners.
5 Explain three reasons why some people consider that prisons in the UK are not effective.

What do you think? AO3

6 **a** Draw up a list of pros and cons about sending children (up to the age of seventeen) to secure children's homes.
   b Looking at all the pros and cons, do you think it is right to send child offenders to secure children's homes?

Capital punishment

What crime would society consider to be so bad that the offender has to forfeit their right to life?

In the past, the death penalty could be awarded for what we would consider to be quite trivial acts. The Waltham Black Act (1723) listed 50 capital offences such as:

● forgery of birth, baptism and marriage certificates

● **arson**

● attempted murder of parents

● picking a pocket of more than one shilling (about £35 today).

Since that time, various reforms of the law reduced the list to murder (including abortion and **infanticide**) until capital punishment was abolished in 1965 (the 'Murder (Abolition of Death Penalty) Act' was passed for a trial period and confirmed in 1969). But **treason** and **piracy** remained on the statute books as capital offences until they were removed in 1988.

In Europe the death penalty has been abolished (with the exception of Belarus) but many countries retain its use, including:

● China   ● North Korea

● India   ● Saudi Arabia

● Iran   ● Singapore

● Iraq   ● Taiwan

● Japan   ● the USA (only in certain states).

Although murder is the major reason for the use of capital punishment, other capital offences include: rape of underage children, treason, **adultery** and selling illegal drugs.

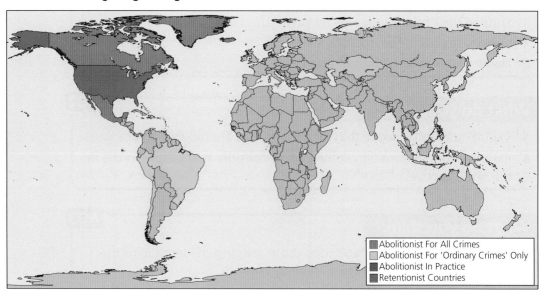

Abolitionist For All Crimes
Abolitionist For 'Ordinary Crimes' Only
Abolitionist In Practice
Retentionist Countries

▲ Map of the world showing the abolitionist (no capital punishment) and retentionist (have capital punishment) countries.

Ethical arguments for capital punishment

The true story of Leopold and Loeb

Nathan Leopold (nineteen) and Richard Loeb (eighteen) were close friends who both came from well-to-do Chicago families. Both were brilliant academically: Leopold went to university at the age of fifteen and Loeb at fourteen. Each of them had carried out **petty crimes** but they wanted to accomplish the perfect crime, which would make the whole of Chicago take notice. They decided they would kidnap and murder a child, and also demand a large ransom. They spent hours making their plans.

On 21 May 1924 they went looking for their victim. Loeb spotted fourteen-year-old Bobby Franks, his cousin and the son of a wealthy businessman. They persuaded him to get into their hired car where they bludgeoned him to death with a chisel. However, when they buried him in a remote spot, Leopold's glasses fell off. By tracing the ownership of the glasses, the police were able to identify the killers. Leopold and Loeb confessed to their crime on 31 May.

The public were horrified by the cold-blooded murder and it seemed they would both be hanged.

However, the families of Loeb and Leopold had hired Clarence Darrow, a well-known and respected lawyer. He was strongly opposed to the death penalty and was also influenced by modern psychology, which suggested that all our actions are the result of upbringing and environment. He argued that crime is almost always the result of a mental disorder and even though the two young men were not insane, they were not fully in control of their actions. Much to the amazement of the prosecution, the judge was persuaded by Darrow's argument, and the two were sentenced to 99 years' imprisonment for kidnap and murder.

Loeb was later killed in prison by an inmate; Leopold was released on parole in 1958 and died of a heart attack in 1971.

Retribution

For the retributivist, the outcome of the Leopold and Loeb case was completely wrong for a number of reasons:

- Leopold and Loeb had absolutely no respect for the life and dignity of Bobby Franks and for the law of the land from which they benefitted. In planning to kill the child, both had forfeited their right to live.

- The judge's decision failed to take into account the terrible loss experienced by the victim's family. Bobby's murder was cold and callous, and execution of the two killers would have helped Bobby's family to see that justice had been done; this would have helped them come to terms with their loss.

- Capital punishment is a sign from society that it recognises the value and dignity of human life. In the Old Testament, it states that: 'Whoever sheds human blood, by humans shall their blood be shed; for in the image of God has God made mankind' (Genesis 9.6). Therefore executing the guilty person shows how much society values the sanctity of God-given human life. Failing to execute the guilty person would suggest that what they did was not so wrong, and that the innocent person's life is not so special.

Deterrence

Another criticism made against the Loeb and Leopold case was that society was now sending out a signal that abduction and cold-blooded murder were not morally terrible. If the judge had sentenced them to be hanged he would have sent out a powerful message that crimes of this kind would not be tolerated. This, in turn, would deter future potential killers and rapists.

Furthermore, as John Stuart Mill argued, the death penalty warns future offenders that terrible crime does not pay. Failure of the state to administer the ultimate punishment would therefore give the criminal an unfair advantage over those law-abiding citizens who recognise the rights and dignity of other citizens.

Protection

There have been many cases where a dangerous criminal has been given parole from prison and then gone on to commit another horrendous crime. Prison is expensive and not always reliable protection against dangerous people such as Leopold and Loeb, so the death penalty completely ensures that society is rid of these types of people.

Reform

The death penalty does not remove the opportunity for the offender to express remorse. By accepting that they must be executed, the offender acknowledges that what they have done is very wrong.

Leopold and Loeb confessed their guilt, so by their own admission they were accepting that they should have been executed.

▲ HMP Belfast, Crumlin Road jail, 2016.

Ethical arguments against capital punishment

Abolitionists (those against capital punishment) argue that fundamentally capital punishment is contrary to the values of a civilised country. Article 5 of the United Nations' Declaration of Human Rights sums this up well, when it says that everyone has the 'right not to be subjected to torture or to cruel, inhuman or degrading punishment'.

Retribution

Many people consider the judge was right to sentence Loeb and Leopold to imprisonment and not execution because had he used capital punishment, the state would have been morally no better than the two killers. They believe that executing a person in cold blood (very different from killing in the heat of battle) is an act of cruelty motivated by revenge not the desire for justice. Many Christians agree because Jesus taught, in the Sermon on the Mount, that an 'eye for an eye' was wrong and Christians should love their enemies. So, even if someone has done something terrible, that does not mean the state has the right to kill them. The sixth commandment in the Old Testament (do not kill) may have allowed capital punishment, but Jesus' teaching aimed for a higher ideal to respect everyone – even criminals. According to Jesus' new teaching on the sixth commandment the state should not use killing as punishment.

Abolitionists also reject capital punishment for retributive reasons because of lack of mental control or **diminished responsibility**. Clarence Darrow used diminished responsibility to defend Leopold and Loeb against execution for their cold-blooded murder of Bobby Franks because no ordinary person would act in this way. He made the point that their actions were the result of their genes and upbringing, over which they only had limited control. In his summing up Darrow argued:

> The principal thing to remember is that we are all the products of heredity and environment, that we have little or no control, as individuals, over ourselves, and that criminals are like the rest of us in that regard.

Deterrence

The argument for capital punishment as deterrence is a strong one, but there is very little proof that it does actually deter would-be murderers or rapists (where these crimes are capital offences) from committing capital offences. Loeb and Leopold were not deterred from kidnapping and murdering a child, and they knew if they were caught they could be executed. Many crimes are committed in the heat of the moment when the thought of execution is not a consideration.

Protection

Life in prison protects society against a dangerous criminal just as effectively as execution. While it is true that keeping someone in prison for life is very expensive, it is equally important that the state is seen to be acting in a humane manner towards everyone. In the story of the adulterous woman (John 8.1–11), her accusers ask Jesus whether she should be executed by stoning for her adultery as the law demanded. Jesus' answer was, 'Let any one of you who is without sin be the first to throw a stone at her.' None of her accusers acted. So, as no one is perfect, the state cannot make the ultimate judgement by taking away someone's life.

Reform

The death penalty does not give the offender the opportunity for repentance. Leopold was released from prison a changed person and lived a normal life. If he had been executed, he wouldn't have had the chance to reform his life.

What do you know? | AO1

1 Briefly summarise the Leopold and Loeb case.
2 Give two retributive reasons and two deterrent reasons for capital punishment.
3 What does Article 5 of the United Nations' Declaration of Human Rights state about punishment?

What do you understand? | AO2

4 Explain briefly why some people think that retribution does not justify capital punishment.
5 Explain why some people think that prison is preferable to capital punishment.

What do you think? | AO3

6 Find out more about diminished responsibility. Do you think it is right to reduce someone's punishment if they were upset or angry or drunk when they committed the crime, or were badly educated?

Essay practice

'The aim of punishment is to help someone to become a better person.' Do you agree? Give reasons for your answer. Show that you have considered more than one point of view.

2.3 Prejudice, discrimination and freedom

What is prejudice?

A prejudice is a belief that is biased against a certain group of people based on little or no evidence and is often irrational. Prejudices are often based on stereotypes; these are simplified generalisations about a group, which are often based on faulty knowledge. Prejudices often lead to discrimination, the unfavourable and unfair treatment of a person or group. So, together prejudice and discrimination can cause great suffering, loss of human dignity and violation of human rights.

Starter
Why do people value freedom?

What causes prejudice?

There are many complex causes of prejudice. Upbringing, culture, religion, political beliefs, morality and class all combine to create one's attitude to other people. Often just knowing about one's prejudices and discussing them openly is enough to make sure that they are not used to discriminate against other people.

But there are other factors that can escalate these prejudices and create social tensions and even violence. These factors might include:

● **Threat**: feeling threatened by the loss of jobs, homes and a way of life caused by outsiders such as immigrants.

● **Fear**: fear of different customs, behaviour and moral standards. This kind of fear is called a phobia. **Xenophobia** is the fear of foreigners and **homophobia** is the fear of gay and lesbian people.

● **Ideology**: belief that there are certain ideals which are correct and which shouldn't be compromised. For example, nationalists believe that nations have developed a certain way of life that makes society harmonious and happy. Nationalists argue that their society must be protected against unpatriotic influences. Nationalism, as well as religion, has often led to sexism, racism and classism.

> The **holocaust** is an example of an ideology that led to extreme racism. The holocaust was the systematic extermination of Jews by the Nazis in the Second World War (1939–45). The Nazis believed that they should 'cleanse' society of Jews whom they blamed for Germany's lack of economic success. From 1942 onwards Jews were transported to concentration camps and then executed.

How does prejudice affect society?

Not only does prejudice create tensions between people, but when these views are entrenched in society they can cause:

- **violence and harassment** such as murder, assaults, attacks on property and abusive language

- **unfair employment and earnings** such as unequal pay, lack of interviews for employment, restrictions on positions of responsibility

- **poor housing and living conditions** such as being offered inferior accommodation, living in overcrowded homes and deprived areas in cities or towns

- **inferior education** such as low expectations for children from a certain class and ethnic background.

Institutionalised discrimination is discrimination by society against certain people, which is not always intentional. In areas such as housing, health care, education, employment and wealth, minorities find themselves disadvantaged not because any one person or group is being consciously prejudiced but because laws and traditions fail to take into account the needs of these minorities.

For example, certain jobs may be thought more suitable for men than women. The army until recently did not place women in the front line of battle because it was generally thought they were not suited to the role. It wasn't that individual soldiers were necessarily sexist, but the army as an institution was.

Institutionalised racism came dramatically into the public consciousness with the unprovoked and racially motivated murder of the teenager Stephen Lawrence.

The Stephen Lawrence Case

Stephen Lawrence was a black British eighteen-year-old from Plumstead, south east London. He excelled at running, and studying technology, English and physics at school, he hoped to become an architect. On the evening of 22 April 1993, he was travelling home late with a friend, Duwayne Brooks, when they were surrounded by five or six white youths. Duwayne thought they said a racist insult to Stephen before forcing him to the ground and fatally stabbing him twice. Stephen and Duwayne tried to run away but Stephen collapsed after a few metres. An ambulance was called but Stephen was already dead.

Although many locals came forward with information about possible suspects and eye witnesses said it was an unprovoked attack, the police did not make any arrests until two weeks later. The suspects were well known to the police for their violence and criminal activity. Later it emerged that the lead investigator had failed to arrest the suspects because he didn't know the law of reasonable suspicion. Then when the arrests and charges of murder were finally made, the charges were rejected by the Crown Prosecution Service because the evidence was insufficient.

The Lawrence family were not convinced that all the relevant information had been presented in court and in April 1994 initiated a private prosecution. This was not successful and in 1996 the judge said there was still not enough evidence to convict.

However, in 1997 the *Daily Mail* decided something had to be done and ran a headline that accused the five suspects of being murderers. The public were outraged that Stephen's killers had not been brought to justice. The Home Secretary commissioned Sir William Macpherson to carry out a report on the handling of the case. The Macpherson Report (1999) revealed serious flaws in the police's routine processes and their handling of the evidence; some police officers had deliberately withheld crucial evidence. The motivation appeared to be racist. In 2013 this was confirmed when a former undercover police officer revealed that he was often put under considerable pressure to undermine the credibility of the Lawrence family's campaign.

In 2006 the BBC broadcast a documentary that raised new questions about the Lawrence case and in 2011 two of the suspects were arrested based on new forensic evidence which showed that they had traces of Stephen's DNA and hair on their clothing. They were convicted of murder and given life imprisonments in 2012.

Stephen's life and tragic death have inspired books and films reflecting on his life and racism in Britain. Buildings have been named after him and an architectural prize awarded in his memory. The 22nd of April is Stephen Lawrence Day. The Stephen Lawrence Charitable Trust is a national educational charity committed to the advancement of social justice.

The Macpherson Report has been called 'one of the most important moments in the modern history of criminal justice in Britain'. It has changed attitudes to racism and to institutions such as the police, and instigated changes in the law to tackle institutionalised prejudice and discrimination in many different areas of British life.

Institutionalised discrimination means that the structures of society make it impossible for there to be true equality between races, classes and sexes. As in all forms of social prejudice and discrimination, what is at stake is the loss of individual freedom and happiness.

Freedom

> *Over himself, over his own body and mind, the individual is sovereign.*
>
> J.S. Mill, *On Liberty*

One of the most influential books on the nature of freedom was written by John Stuart Mill in the middle of the nineteenth century and is called *On Liberty*. Mill's argument is that we value freedom because each person is the best judge of his or her life and as we are all different, society should give us the maximum amount of freedom so we can choose to live as we wish. In the famous quotation above, Mill is arguing that each individual should be the ruler or 'sovereign' of his or her body and mind. Mill's **liberty principle** has become enormously influential because it seems obvious that societies are most harmonious when their citizens can freely choose what kind of lifestyle they wish to live and tolerate lifestyles different from their own.

However, Mill also realised that the liberty principle would have to be modified to stop people causing harm to others. That is why Mill argued that the state should limit a person's liberty at times to reduce harm. Mill expressed the harm principle as follows:

> *The only purpose for which power can be rightfully exercised over any member of a civilised community, against his will, is to prevent harm to others.*
>
> J.S. Mill, *On Liberty*

Activity

Tolerance Terrace

Three families live in a terrace next door to each other. The houses are reasonably private but noise travels through the walls and the gardens are only separated by thin fences.

22 Tolerance Terrace	23 Tolerance Terrace	24 Tolerance Terrace

Mary and William Smith are elderly and live a quiet life, getting up early, tending their garden and going to bed early. They have been married for 60 years and strongly disapprove of cohabitation and believe couples should be married before having sex and bringing up children. William can get cross easily and will tell people bluntly what he thinks of them.	Amanda Brown and Susan Griffith are a lesbian couple in their late twenties who live together with their two children aged three and two. The children are often restless at night. Amanda has opted to remain at home to look after the children while Susan goes to work as a doctor at the local hospital. The children play in the garden in the day time and make a noise.	Richard and Anita Shepherd are a married couple who have both been divorced. They have a sixteen-year-old son of their own and a nineteen-year-old daughter from Anita's former relationship. They have a fairly relaxed attitude to their children's lives. The son likes to listen to loud rock music and the daughter likes to stay up late chatting to her friends.

In groups, do the following:

a Make a list of all the things that each family might disapprove of.

b Look at your list and decide which things are mental harms.

c Now decide which things in your list are physical harms.

d Discuss how the tensions between the various families might be reduced.

The question is this: at what point is it reasonable to restrict someone's freedom because it interferes with another person's liberty by causing them harm?

We hold these truths to be self-evident, that all men are created equal, that they are endowed by their Creator with certain unalienable rights, that among these are Life, Liberty and the Pursuit of Happiness.

American Declaration of Independence (1776)

Freedom and tolerance of others is the foundation of human rights. Human rights form the foundation of modern constitutions. The creation of the United States of America was founded on the three rights: life, liberty and the pursuit of happiness. After the Second World War, the United Nations created the **Universal Declaration of Human Rights** (1948), which has set the standard for human rights globally, as a 'common standard of achievement for all peoples and all nations'.

The first three articles of the Universal Declaration of Human Rights are as follows:

- **Article 1**: 'All humans are born free and equal in dignity and rights. They are endowed with reason and conscience and should act towards one another in a spirit of brotherhood.'

- **Article 2**: 'Everyone is entitled to all the rights and freedoms set forth in this Declaration, without distinction of any kind, such as race, colour, sex, language, religion or other opinion, national or social origin, property, birth or other status.' Rights extend beyond political boundaries.

- **Article 3**: 'Everyone has the right to life, liberty and security of person.'

Perhaps one of the most significant ideas of the Universal Declaration is that rights are only available to those who in return acknowledge their duties to uphold the rights of others. The Declaration states that 'everyone has duties to the community'. There can be no rights without duties. Perhaps your discussion of Tolerance Terrace led you to the same conclusion.

Freedom of speech

As we have seen on page 99, Socrates refused to stop teaching the young men of Athens to think and question things for themselves. As a result, he was regarded as a dangerous trouble maker and sentenced to death. Socrates' point was that without freedom of speech, democracy would not function – no one would be able to express their views openly, debate them and defend them.

So, the question is: in a liberal democratic society are there limits on what people may say about each other?

▲ What are the limits of free speech?

One limit is speaking and writing untruths about someone, which causes them harm. Speaking untruths about someone in public is called slander and is a crime punishable by law. Writing something that is untrue about someone is called libel and is also a crime punishable by law.

More problematic are the limits society places on the press, i.e. print, broadcast and internet. A liberal society is often judged by the amount of freedom the press is permitted in making comments about the government, public figures, laws and so on. But are there some matters that the press should not be allowed to report and comment on?

- Matters of national security
- The private lives of celebrities
- The private lives of ordinary people
- Classified information which could be of national interest
- Political opinions

Discuss

Should the government have more control over the internet?

The biggest challenge to freedom of speech and freedom of the press is the internet. Whereas in the past the authors of television and newspaper articles could be traced and the person presenting their ideas held responsible, the internet means that it is often very difficult to track down the author of a libellous blog or website.

Freedom of action

Freedom of speech is also referred to as freedom of expression. Freedom of expression is not just the freedom to express views but also to have the opportunity to perform actions freely; doing things we wish to do is fundamentally important to living a happy life. This is why many argue that just expressing your views is not enough if physically you are imprisoned or confined to your house or not allowed to travel outside your town or country.

As with freedom of speech there are also limits to freedom of action and these limits are often controversial and hard to define.

For example, it is relatively straightforward to limit where a toddler might travel. It would be a very bad parent who allowed their small child to wander unsupervised along the pavement and possibly into the road. This would not only cause a risk to the child's life but to road users. But as the child grows up parents know they have to reduce their control and allow their child greater freedom, even if there are still risks.

So, at what point are we justified in intervening in someone's life if we think they are at risk to themselves or of causing harm to others?

The issue is much discussed among those who work with the very old and those with disabilities and mental health problems. Carers have to balance the right to freedom of action of those in their care against the harm caused before intervening with physical restraint. '**Interventions**', as they are called, may only be used as a last resort, but sometimes the intervention comes too late and the person has badly harmed him or herself or someone else.

Freedom of action is an important way in which ordinary people can express their political views. A democracy allows people to gather, hold meetings, conduct marches, strike and make public protests against the state. Martin Luther King used some of these actions to show those in authority that the law was unjust, racist and prejudiced and had to be reformed. Of course, he also took risks. People died, many were injured and many considered what he did to be morally wrong. But, imagine a society where protests of this kind were completely forbidden. This was the case in East Germany before unification with West Germany in 1989. The job of the East German security service police force, the Stasi, was to spy on everyone to ensure that no one acted against the state.

▲ In the film *The Lives of Others* (2006), the Stasi secretly monitor the life of anyone they think might be a threat to the state. How much information do you think the state should be allowed to acquire about its citizens?

Freedom of belief

For a liberal democratic society to flourish it has to allow all its members the freedom to believe openly what they wish, even if those beliefs are anti-liberal. The alternative would be a society as described in George Orwell's novel *Nineteen Eighty-Four* where the thought-police control people's beliefs to conform to the ideology of the state. This would be like being one of the prisoners in Plato's Parable of the Cave, where the prisoners think that what they believe is the truth but they have no way of testing it. We have also seen in the philosophy of David Hume that he also passionately believed that we should have the freedom to challenge our own beliefs and the beliefs of others.

Freedom of belief is also known as **intellectual freedom**. Intellectual freedom allows a person to develop their own religious, political and moral values. In a multicultural society this is very important as it allows everyone to live the kinds of life they value and to accept that there will be differences of views and opinions.

It is important to have freedom of belief so there can be open and honest debate. This is especially important in politics but also at universities, where students should have the opportunity to explore and analyse ideas without being told what to believe.

Everyone has the right to freedom of opinion and expression; this right includes freedom to hold opinions without interference and to seek, receive and impart information and ideas through any media and regardless of frontiers.

Universal Declaration of Human Rights, Article 19

But as with freedom of speech and action there are also limits to freedom of belief. Consider the following:

- Should schools and parents restrict children's access to the internet and limit web searches?

- Should public libraries and internet sites be allowed to contain books and articles that are racist, sexist and homophobic (anti-gay) and designed to stir up hate?

- Is it acceptable for comedians to poke fun at religions and make anti-religious jokes?

- Should teachers be allowed to express their own religious, moral and political beliefs through their teaching?

Censorship of belief has long been problematic. In 1960 D.H. Lawrence's novel *Lady Chatterley's Lover* (1928) was the cause of a major legal debate. Some people thought it should be banned as it includes language and descriptions that are sexually explicit and were therefore thought to have the potential to corrupt public morality, while others argued that adults should make up their own minds whether they wished to read the novel. The book was published. On the other hand, films that contain extreme violence or pornography are considered to be emotionally and morally harmful and so they are censored. The question remains: what is harmful and where should the censorship line be drawn?

What do you know? — AO1

1 What is slander?
2 What is libel?
3 What does 'freedom of the press' mean?
4 In a care home what is an 'intervention'?

What do you understand? — AO2

5 Explain why freedom of action is important.
6 Explain why intellectual freedom is important for the individual.
7 Give three reasons why censorship is good.

What do you think? — AO3

8 Find out about a country where it is illegal to criticise the leader (the president or monarch).

   a Describe what happens to those who do criticise the leader in this country.

   b Set out the advantages and disadvantages of making it illegal to criticise the leader of a country.

   c Do you think we should be encouraged to criticise the leaders of our country?

Treatment of the marginalised in society

The marginalised members of society are often those who have been discriminated against through no fault of their own or because they have failed to conform to society's standards and their particular needs have been forgotten.

The central moral question is how to treat those who are marginalised because of society's prejudices and those who are marginalised because of their failure to be good members of society.

Who are the marginalised?

Those who are marginalised because of their failure to be good members of society include:

- **The poor** because they are sometimes considered to be spongers, lazy, thieves and anti-social. Although this might apply to some, many are poor through illness, poor education, poor upbringing and misfortune.

- **Drug abusers and alcoholics** are marginalised because in order to feed their habit they break the law by stealing and threatening others and being abusive. While many drug abusers might have chosen this way of life, others fall into it out of a sense of hopelessness or misfortune (some people experiment with drugs and then find themselves addicted).

Those who are marginalised because of society's prejudices include:

- **Disabled people** are sometimes treated as if they are less than human, lacking in intelligence and unable to be part of society. In reality, disability covers a wide range of conditions and the disabled can participate in society in many different ways.

- **Women** are sometimes treated as if their only role is to be mothers and carry out domestic chores. In reality, many women choose to be mothers as well as taking on paid employment in all spheres of society.

- **Immigrants**, in particular economic migrants (those seeking jobs because work is more plentiful here than in their own countries, such as India, Bangladesh, Poland, etc.), are treated with mistrust as they are perceived as taking jobs away from locals and receiving benefits. In reality, many immigrants greatly benefit society with their skills and knowledge.

- **Ethnic minorities** are often treated as a threat to national life and culture but, in reality, ethnic groups can enrich society culturally, spiritually and socially.

Moral issues

The central moral challenge is to break down prejudices by becoming aware of them. Often when people realise that they hold a prejudice and understand the reason why it unfairly discriminates, they change their minds. However, this can take time and effort on the part of pressure groups, campaigners, religious leaders and legal reformers.

A difficult and controversial means of bringing about change for those who are marginalised is through **positive action** or **affirmative action**. Positive action involves acting in favour of a marginalised group in preference to those who have not been marginalised. For example, some political parties have favoured choosing more women to become Members of Parliament to compensate for the many men who have traditionally occupied this role. A business might actively favour those from ethnic minorities to develop an inclusive workforce. Universities might favour students from poor working-class backgrounds to widen their access to higher education.

> A year after Congress passed far-reaching rights legislation forbidding public segregation, President Lyndon B. Johnson made the following statement which implicitly justifies the use of affirmative action in the process of combating racism and making society a fairer place:
>
> *But freedom is not enough. You do not wipe away the scars of centuries by saying: now you are free to go where you want, and do as you desire, and choose the leaders you please.*
>
> *You do not take a person who, for years, has been hobbled by chains and liberate him, bring him up to the starting line of a race and then say, 'you are free to compete with all the others,' and still justly believe that you have been completely fair.*
>
> Lyndon B. Johnson *'To Fulfil These Rights'*, Commencement Address at Howard University, 4 June 1965

What do you understand? **AO2**

1 Explain why some people become marginalised in society.
2 Why do the marginalised often suffer from prejudice and discrimination?
3 Explain what is meant by positive action (or affirmative action).

What do you think? **AO3**

4 Many people think positive action is unfair and does more harm than good. Make a list of the points for and against it.

Essay practice

'Freedom of speech almost always causes harm.' Do you agree? Give reasons for your answer. Show that you have considered more than one point of view.

2.4 The environment

Starter
Why should humans be held morally responsible for the environment?

Environmental crisis

▲ Hurricane Irma caused huge devastation in 2017. Are these hurricanes becoming more common because of human misuse of the environment?

Many people today argue that we are in a state of environmental crisis. In 2006, Al Gore, the vice-president of the USA, produced a controversial film called *An Inconvenient Truth*. Over ten years later its sequel *An Inconvenient Sequel: Truth to Power* (2017) follows up on Gore's attempt to persuade governments that global warming is a reality and not fiction. Just before the release of the film many world powers had signed the Paris Climate Agreement (2016) committing their countries to invest in renewable energy.

Not everyone is convinced there is an environmental crisis and not everyone is clear what the moral principles are behind the environmental issues.

Those who are convinced that there is an urgent need to address an environmental crisis are called **environmentalists**; those who think that there are environmental moral issues to address but who argue that there is not a crisis, are called **environmental sceptics**.

Summary of some of central environmental issues

Humans have become increasingly aware that the Earth and their way of life is being threatened by environmental crisis. The crisis affects all humans, animals and other life forms on the planet.

- **Climate change** is causing extremes of hot and cold weather conditions. This causes a rise in ocean levels, leading to land erosion and hurricanes, both of which have led to loss of life and devastation of communities.

- The use of fossil fuels and deforestation are adding to the **greenhouse gases** in the atmosphere and contributing to climate change.

- CFCs (from fridges, aerosols and so on) are **depleting the ozone layer.** This layer protects humans and animals from dangerous rays from the sun, which cause skin cancers.

- The **use of fossil or natural fuels** causes pollution. When these fuels run out, the modern way of life that depends on electricity and fuel for transport will no longer be possible. This will lead to a breakdown in modern ways of living.

- The rise in **world population** increases industrial processes. This leads to greater need for fuel to transport goods, greater food production and more intensive farming methods. Great demand for meat from cattle produces high levels of methane (a greenhouse gas), which is released when cattle eat grass.

- **Pollution** due to nuclear waste, industrial and household waste degrades the soil and makes the land impossible for humans and animals to use.

Between the environmentalists and the environmental sceptics there is a great range of moral views about what duties we have to the environment. It is usual to arrange their ideas from shallow ecological ethical views to deep ecological ethical views of the environment.

- **Shallow ecologists** believe that we act out of self-interest and that our duties to the environment stem from the fact that we don't want to be the losers in the ecological crisis.

- **Deep ecologists** believe that humans and the environment are deeply connected and so we have a duty to deal with any environmental crisis because as human beings we have a major part to play in the future of the world's welfare.

Between these two extremes lies a whole range of different moral arguments as to how we should treat the environment and why; these include a wide variety of differing religious and non-religious views.

Ethics: a debate about human treatment of the environment

Read the following imaginary interview. Who do you think is the deep ecologist and who is the shallow ecologist?

▲ 'Saving the Planet' television debate.

In the TV studio Alec Burgess, the interviewer watches the teleprompter as the music of Saving the Planet *dies away. In armchairs either side of him are his two guests, Catherine Catastrophe and Steve Sceptic.*

Alec: Good evening and welcome to the last in our series on *Saving the Planet*. In previous programmes we have presented the issues of greenhouse gases and their effects on the ozone layer, the extremes of weather conditions, the melting of the polar cap and rising sea levels, the use of fossil fuels and depletion of natural resources – and much more. But what we haven't yet debated is why these issues are morally controversial.

In the studio this evening I have two experts who represent very different views about the ethical implications of the facts. Catherine Catastrophe is a journalist who has interviewed hundreds of scientists and represents the environmentalist pressure group Stop! Steve Sceptic is a scientist who represents the environmental pressure group Caution.

Catherine, what are the central moral issues, from the point of view of Stop?

Catherine: Thank you, Alec. Our message is very simple. The planet is on the edge of environmental catastrophe and unless we act now, we won't have a future. A few years ago Al Gore, the vice-president of the United States of America, produced a film *An Inconvenient Truth* (2006) which many people thought was just scaremongering. But so much of what he predicted has come true. We have seen more extreme events in weather conditions, such as hurricanes Nadine (2012) and Irma (2017). Hundreds of lives have been lost and communities have been devastated.

Alec: No one would disagree that these are terrible events but as they are natural, why should these be moral issues?

Catherine: The point is that humans are almost entirely the reason why there has been change because since the industrial revolution in the late eighteenth century the human impact on the environment has clearly been the cause of the catastrophes you referred to in your introduction. Humans are morally to blame and we are responsible for doing something about it. We have a duty to our children and to future generations to act now and change how we behave for their sake. If we don't, then I don't see humans being around on the planet in a few hundred years' time.

Alec: Steve, Catherine speaks with passion and makes her moral position very clear, yet you and your organisation Caution don't agree with her – why?

Steve: I don't agree with her because her science is not accurate and her moral position is weak. Let's begin with the science. I am not a climate change denier, but I do think her explanation that humans are almost entirely responsible for the changes we are experiencing is wrong. The fact is that we don't know whether the present climate change is just a phase the world is going through or whether it is long term. It is too simplistic to put all the blame on humans.

Alec: So, does this mean that we *don't* have any moral duties to the environment?

Steve: I think we very definitely do have duties but these moral duties have to balance one thing against another. For example, supposing we flood a valley and set up a hydro-electric generator station. The good thing about doing this is that it reduces the use of fossil fuels but at the same time it destroys a natural habitat and its ecosystem and perhaps the lifestyle of people who have lived and worked on the land for hundreds of years. Ecosystems are complex and we need to move cautiously and at a local level so we can see what impact we are having.

I don't think Catherine has a moral view of the environment; all she is concerned about is human survival. I, on the other hand, care about the environment for its own sake. What we need to develop are small, sustainable communities that have genuine moral respect for the ecosystem.

Catherine: I don't think Steve fully understands the situation. He thinks we should be thinking about green issues at a local level but this will not bring about the changes needed to save the planet. We need to show governments and multi-national companies (MNCs) that they have

the power to alter the way we behave now. MNCs have got to pay a fair wage to people in a poor or a less economically developed country so that they are not, for example, forced to cut down trees, which causes deforestation. Fewer trees means there is more carbon dioxide in the atmosphere, which causes global warming.

Steve: My problem with Catherine's view is that all she is trying to do is frighten us into action. Real change takes place in small ways at the local level. Teaching people to recycle at home and in the workplace means that they learn to think about their place in the environment and their views on the environment change accordingly. She depicts us as viewers of a disaster movie where the film director allows us to choose the ending. I believe that we are not viewers but participants in the movie, as it were. She talks about looking at the environment as a kind of thing; I think of it as alive – and we humans are just one significant aspect of it.

Alec: I see. So, do you think animals and rocks have just as many moral rights as humans?

Steve: No, but I think non-human animals have a right to be respected and treated fairly. Rocks are part of the ecosystem, so we need to think consciously about how we treat them, along with plants, insects and bacteria. The point is we share the planet; we don't own it.

Catherine: I am not clear why Steve doesn't agree with me. We also think we should be striving for a sustainable planet. We have duties to stop pollution, reduce populations, find alternative forms of power and energy.

Steve: It is not that I disagree with you, Catherine, on these points; it is just that I don't think your moral reasons are valid.

Catherine: What could be more important than making the world habitable for us now and in the future? We have overcome slavery, we have campaigned for women's rights, fought for gay and lesbian rights and now we must fight for the environment. These examples must surely mean that I have a sound moral basis for our campaign.

Alec: Steve, in a sentence, sum up your moral environmental principle.

Steve: We must treat every aspect of the world with great respect because we are part of it and depend on it.

Alec: There we must leave it. Catherine and Steve both think they have an environmental ethic, but they have a fundamental difference of opinion about what it is. I leave you, the viewers, to work out what it is and whether you side more with Catherine or Steve – or perhaps neither of them. Remember, this issue is not trivial, at stake is 'Saving the Planet'.

All the characters and their pressure groups in this interview are invented, but their views are widely held by different people.

▲ Former vice president and environmental activist Al Gore addresses the Investor Summit on Climate Risk at the United Nations in New York City, 2016.

What do you know? — AO1

1 Give three examples of environmental crises that are threatening the Earth and human existence.
2 Who is Al Gore?
3 What is the Paris Climate Agreement?

What do you understand? — AO2

4 Explain what environmental sceptics believe.
5 Explain what environmentalists believe.
6 Explain the main difference between shallow and deep ecology.

What do you think? — AO3

7 Who do you agree with more in the TV debate above: Catherine or Steve? Give reasons to support your answer.

Environmental ethics

Although environmental ethics may be described as shallow and deep, in practice there are degrees of difference from one to the other. Here are three views to consider.

Ethical beliefs about the treatment of the environment

shallow ecology

Those who hold a shallow ecological ethical position believe that ethics are human-centred. **Utilitarians**, for example, believe that if the best way of behaving is to promote the **greatest happiness of the greatest number** of people, then the main reason for treating the environment with care is because humans don't want to suffer the negative effects of global warming, pollution, lack of energy resources and food, etc.

However, many utilitarians also argue that we should take into account the suffering of *all* creatures capable of feeling pain and ensure that non-human animals as well as humans are treated with care and respect. Some utilitarians argue that non-human animals which are more conscious of pain (such as apes and dolphins) should be given greater priority over those that are less conscious of pain (such as birds, fish and insects).

medium ecology

In the middle ecological ethical position are the views held by many **Christians**. The Christian view focuses on God as the creator of every aspect of creation. All creation is good and purposeful because God has created it (Genesis 1.10). God commands humans to look after the creation on his behalf as his **stewards** (Genesis 1.28). Importantly, humans do not own the world but maintain it for God. The promise or covenant between God and people is that he will protect them if they respect the land and maintain the natural order (Genesis 12.1–3). Finally, humans have a duty to restore any damage they have caused to the world in preparation for God's final judgement (Romans 8.18–23).

deep ecology

There are religious and non-religious deep ecological ethical views. For example, **Buddhists** believe that as every aspect of the world is connected to each other, humans must not think they have a superior place in it. According to the principle of **karma** if we deliberately harm any aspect of the environment this will have negative effects on the world and on ourselves, which we cannot calculate.

Non-religious deep ecologists think of the planet as being alive as a vast organism. One writer uses the word **Gaia** (the ancient Greek goddess of the earth) to describe all the processes that govern the world. Some think that if we don't respect Gaia then it is possible that we and many other species may die out. One way of living in harmony with Gaia is to create small, sustainable communities which emit very few greenhouse gases and use non-fossil fuels for energy and heating.

What do you understand? AO2

1 Explain why many utilitarians are 'shallow ecologists'.

2 Explain the Christian teaching on stewardship and the environment.

3 Explain the Buddhist teaching on karma and the environment.

4 What do some deep ecologists mean by 'Gaia'?

What do you think? AO3

5 Find out about the philosopher **Arne Naess** (1912–2009). Outline his ideas and suggestions for living in a more ecologically ethical way. Do you agree with environmental ethics?

Ethical treatment of animals

The treatment of animals, or more precisely non-human animals (for humans are also animals), has become a significant issue in environmental ethics for two reasons.

First, farming of animals for human consumption can alter **biodiversity** (developing many different animal and plant species). Biodiversity is good because animals depend on each other in the food chain; if there are too many or too few of a certain species then this can upset the balance. For example, cows excrete methane, which is a greenhouse gas. If no one ate beef then smaller numbers of cattle would be bred and a major source of greenhouse gas would therefore be removed.

Secondly, increasingly people consider that non-human animals should be treated with care and consideration. In the past, philosophers such as **René Descartes** (1596–1650) thought animals had no souls or consciousness and were little more than machines. They would therefore not be able to feel pain and we would be justified in using them as we wish.

Animals have less reason than man ... They have none at all.

Many people today think Descartes was wrong. Animals do feel pain and so to cause an animal unnecessary pain is morally wrong. The utilitarian philosopher **Jeremy Bentham** (1748–1832) famously stated about animals: 'The question is not "Can animals *reason*?", not "Can they *talk*?", but "Can they *suffer*?"'

The question is not 'Can animals reason?', not 'Can they talk?', but 'Can they suffer?'

But even if we think that animals shouldn't suffer unnecessarily, is it right that animals should be used in medical experiments (to test drugs for humans); be used for human entertainment (in zoos, circuses and as pets); be eaten by humans for food; be used as organ and tissue donors for humans?

So, what are the moral arguments for being a meat-eater and for being a vegetarian?

Although, in theory, we could eat animals if they were well looked after and slaughtered painlessly, on balance, the suffering caused to animals outweighs the pleasure we gain in eating them.

Humans are biologically designed to eat meat so, as long as we don't deliberately cause them harm and we kill them as painlessly as possible, eating meat is acceptable.

Each year 8 billion animals are killed in the United States food industry – that is 16,000 per minute. We don't need to eat animals to survive and if the only reason we do so is because we enjoy the taste of eating their flesh, then the considerable suffering of animals through intensive factory farming and fishing is not justified.

Eating meat is indeed pleasurable, as it is for non-human carnivore animals to eat meat. It is misleading to quote the vast quantity of animals killed for human consumption as there are a lot of humans in the world. It is true we don't need to eat meat to survive but there is more to life than mere existence.

If it is morally repellent to think of eating a human (except in extreme circumstances) then it is also morally repellent to eat an animal. Generally, we don't eat animals we think of as our pets because we have a relationship with them. This means that we eat the animals we do eat because we think we are superior to them; that is arrogant and wrong.

While it is true that we tend not to eat animals that are our pets, this is not because we think they have the same moral status as us. In some ways we are morally superior to animals. Animals do not have the same abilities to make moral decisions and we don't hold them morally responsible if, for example, they kill another animal. Under law, it is the human owner of a dog who savages another dog or a human who is legally responsible and can be charged for criminal damage.

Vegetarianism is good for the planet and for a healthy lifestyle.

But vegetarians still drink animal milk and eat eggs. Animals are still suffering because of the human need for animal products. The only logical way forward to end this is for vegetarians to become vegans.

Ethical treatment of the material world

We have seen that the ethical motivations for caring for the material world depend on whether you hold a shallow or deep ecology view. However, in practice, both views are concerned with **conservation** or the management and care of natural resources, and protecting them from damage and loss. This can be achieved in a number of practical ways.

Practical ways of treating the material world

Political agreements Political agreements have been established through a number of **summits** (meetings between heads of government). The **Kyoto Summit** (1997) set targets for lower gas emissions by implementing incentives or 'carbon credits'. The **Copenhagen Summit** (December 2009) developed the idea that nations have to think of themselves belonging to global communities if the effects of global warming are to be tackled effectively.

The **Paris Climate Agreement** (2016) has been the biggest meeting to date of nations agreeing to reduce global temperature rises. One of the aims was to 'adapt to the adverse impacts of climate change and foster climate resilience and low greenhouse gas emissions development, in a manner that does not threaten food production'. In some countries this has already led to an aim to ban all petrol and diesel vehicles within the next 25 years. For example, in the UK, Oxford is planning on creating a Zero Emissions Zone by banning all petrol and diesel cars from the city from 2020 and from then on will only allow electric cars.

Thinking green It has generally been found that the best way of changing attitudes to conservation is not through major political campaigns which focus on large-scale environmental issues but rather on local small-scale changes in social attitudes and personal behaviour. Getting people to 'think green' might be achieved through environment education at school; encouraging people to recycle waste at home and in the workplace; reducing fuel consumption; using alternative forms of power (such as solar panels); building better insulated houses and so on.

Discuss

It is more important that we deal with green issues at a local level than leave it to governments to deal with.

Many of the moral issues have already been covered in the debate between Catherine and Steve at the start of this chapter. You might like to go over what they said and think about the practical issues referred to above. There is, however, one philosophical issue raised by Catherine which needs more thought: do we really have a duty to look after future generations?

Activity

Look at the following statements. Write a short speech that leads up to and ends with **one** of these statements.

- We only have a duty to look after the environment for ourselves because we don't know what people in the future will want.

- We only have a duty to look after the environment for ourselves and our children because we are only responsible for our children and we don't want them to suffer.

- We have a duty to look after the environment for our children and all future generations because it would be morally wrong to make them suffer for our selfishness.

- We have no duty to look after the environment for future generations because we can't be responsible to people who don't yet exist.

Essay practice

'Humans only care about the environment for entirely selfish reasons.' Do you agree? Give reasons for your answer. Show that you have considered more than one point of view.

Index